RWANDA, BLOOD EVERYWHERE AND BEYOND

DESTRUCTION OF THE REFUGEE CAMP OF KATALE

(TRANSLATED AND UPDATED BY THE AUTHOR FROM THE FRENCH VERSION)

EMMANUEL NGIRUWONSANGA

Published by:

FriesenPress

Suite 300 – 852 Fort Street
Victoria, BC, Canada V8W 1H8

www.friesenpress.com

Distributed to the trade by The Ingram Book Company

TABLE OF CONTENTS

DEDICATION

To you, who have survived the Genocide in Rwanda
and the inhumane massacres in the Congo;

To you, who have been my companions along the
road especially through the jungles of the Congo in
the Ex-Republic of Zaire;

To you, who are impassioned for peace in Rwanda
and the countries of the Great Lakes.

EPIGRAPH

"The ultimate tragedy is not the oppression and cruelty by the bad people but the silence over that by the good people" —Dr. Martin Luther King, Jr.

"We must live together as brothers or perish together as fools." —Dr. Martin Luther King, Jr.

"In the end, we will remember not the words of our enemies, but the silence of our friends. —Dr. Martin Luther King, Jr.

"If I were forced to do injustice or suffer it, I would choose the latter." —Socrates

PREFACE

This is not an imaginary story or one invented in any way by the author. The account is based on the testimony of children living in the streets. The two main characters in this book actually lived on the streets of Kigali. This account is not solely based on the testimony of specific street children, but also on observations of their behaviour and analysis as to probable underlying causes of their behaviour. The author formulates hypotheses as to the consequences of such behaviour, barring any intervention. Supporting these hypotheses are examples pulled from the experiences of others who have lived in unbearable situations. They have been included to help the reader understand what really happened in that small and unknown country in the world.

If a Rwandan were to meet a stranger, especially one from the Western world, the first question he would be asked would be: "Are you Hutu or Tutsi?"

He wouldn't be sure how to respond because these two labels have come to convey another connotation in the past decades. Before that time, Rwanda was not well known in the Western world. Those who did know the country thought of it as "the Switzerland of Africa", and with good reason.

Since the actual policy of our country professes the supposed non-existence of ethnic groups, to admit that one is Hutu is to willingly allow oneself to be called a "Genocide perpetrator," a concept that politicians equate with the ethnic group of Hutu. Just a few months ago, a European man, to whom I had told I was Rwandan, commented that we had a wise president.

Immediately I thought of Mr. Kagame, the strong man of Kigali, and the man whose hands are stained with the blood of countless innocent people of Rwanda and the Congo.

"Your President has suffered a great deal," this European man said, "having been in prison for 27 years. How wonderful that, once he became President, he ended the Genocide and didn't even seek revenge on the whites who had incarcerated him."

When I asked him the President's name, he replied without hesitation. "Nelson Mandela."

I found it troubling to have to explain to him that Nelson Mandela was President of the Republic of South Africa. He hadn't stopped the Genocide because the massacres that occurred during the Apartheid were never recognized as Genocide. It was only after I pointed out South Africa on a map that he realized that Rwanda is one of the 55 countries in Africa and that South Africa is one of them and not the continent itself. Rwanda is so small on a Map of the World that all one sees is a little dot surrounded by Lake Victoria or Lake Tanganyika.

Then he told me that the Genocide was better known than Rwanda itself, as was the word *Interahamwe*. This is a sad truth.

This book is the testimony of a child who was orphaned when his father, and subsequently his mother, were killed during the 1996 attacks on Zairian refugee camps by General Kagame—now the incumbent president of Rwanda—and his troops. In those attacks, refugees were hunted down all the way to the borders of what was once known as Zaire. This child walked more than 13,000 km across the huge country of Zaire. On his back, he carried his baby brother, born just hours before his journey began. A real mystery, isn't it? These two boys, returning from the Republic of Zaire—presently the Democratic Republic of the Congo—roamed the streets of Kigali, the Capital of Rwanda, with the other street kids. Everything belonging to their family had already been seized by others coming in from Uganda in 1994 after the Genocide. This was accomplished by intimidation and threats of death by identifying the rightful owners as Interahamwe. When the Genocide began, the oldest boy was only five years old and his little brother had not yet been born. Who can make any sense of all this? Wherein lies the logic of social justice in Rwanda?

The object of this book is to point out one of the sources of the misery that raged in the country of "Good Governance", Rwanda. Likewise, the real heroes of this account should be seen as interpreters of the marginalized class in Rwandan society. Therefore, reference to the collective "we" will refer at times to the two children, sometimes to the marginalized class, and at other times to the Burundian and Rwandan refugees who found themselves in the refugee camps in Zaire along with the author of this testimonial book. This account differs from a history book, even though it integrates and intertwines real facts over a period of four years[1] concerning the systematic destruction of refugee camps from Rwanda, Burundi, and East Congo in 1996. It is neither a work of fiction nor a figment of the imagination. It is a book that documents real testimony accompanied by analysis by the author. Nonetheless, it remains principally an eyewitness account.

My heartfelt thanks go out to these children who agreed to open their broken hearts to expose to me a tumour that gnawed within. I also thank every person from near and far who has accepted to read these notes, to help form an eventual correct copy, and of course to those who translated it from French to English.

Emmanuel Ngiruwonsanga,
Waterloo, Canada. October 5, 2011

---

1 — The manuscript for the book was written in 2000. Since I was still in Rwanda where freedom of speech was not tolerated and still to this day is not tolerated, and the government denied that they had killed Rwandan and Burundian refugees, it would have been suicidal for me to publish a book such as this. Besides, who would have accepted to edit and publish it, since anyone in Rwanda who would have undertaken the task would have been put on a list of "Genocide perpetrators." Being Hutu or Tutsi, they would have been put into prison or lynched.

PART ONE

SURVIVAL IN ZAIRE AS AN ORPHAN

My mother was assassinated in Zaire shortly after my birth. My name is Ntazina. I was born in Zaire, of a mother I never knew. I am four years old (this was in 2000). If my mother had not died so shortly after giving birth to me, she would have undoubtedly named me *Birame* (miraculous one) because of the conditions under which I was born. Since I am not old enough to recount everything that I've seen and lived through, please allow my big brother, who actually became both father and mother to me since the moment of my birth, to relate the story of my life.

At this point, the big brother began his presentation but stipulated that his story must be heard under these terms: "Do not be surprised that I am not an adult. My age has no bearing on my experience. I have many, many years of experience even if, in reality, I am only eleven years old. In my short life, I have been confronted with human wickedness. I ask but one thing of you—that is to be patient with me and tolerant of what I am relating. I may seem too talkative, but please excuse me. Don't forget, I am old! Allow me a short introduction, but I must warn you—it won't be as short as you think. I will not give you too many details but will stick to the essentials. Improvisation will be my style, and whatever pops into my head, I will share with you. Now that you've already forgiven me, I will begin. Believe me, whatever I'm going to tell you, will not be a day to day replay. No, but I will try to tell you everything that I remember. Even though it was a long time ago, I remember almost everything like it was just yesterday. Please don't expect a systematic exposé from me or a child's make-believe story. I promise that I am serious. My name is *Mbazende*, which translates as (upon whom we repute all that has befallen us).

The following account will be that of Mbazende but often interspersed with comments from the author. I invoke your patience and understanding. The child has given his testimony in the local language, Kinyarwanda, and a liberal translation has been made by the writer. In this chapter, he frequently uses the collective "we" which, at times, refers to the two children, at other times to the Mayibobo in general. It may also refer to those suffering hardship, for whom Mbazende is a spokesperson and whose story echoes that of all refugees. He has appointed himself as "a voice for those who have no voice." The analysis and comments in this section serve to describe the miserable state of life and the social inequity that ravages Rwanda today.

I'm an eleven year old orphan. I have been orphaned for four years. I have never had much opportunity in life. You will be able to guess why later. I am a street kid, a *Mayibobo* in my native language. My address, as well as my cell phone number—because everyone needs a cell phone number—is zero, definitely zero. I spend my nights under the bridges of Kigali or under the canopy of high-rises when the police aren't mean and chase me away. I live perched like a bird! My street companions aren't friends in the sense that I would share my food with them, but they are my comrades.

In the Rwandan culture, a name can designate a wish by the parents for that child. It can also shed light on the situation into which the child is born. So the name *Mbazende* also means the child born during the time of a war that interrupted a period of peace. This name raised questions by many Rwandans at the beginning of the so-called Dirty War of October 1st, 1990. Ntazina's name signifies that there was no one there to name him. Normally it is the father who names the child and, in his absence, the mother. Both of Ntazina's parents were already dead. Though Birame was the name that his mother had whispered, it did not hold up legally because his older brother had uttered it publicly, and children do not have the right to name younger siblings. So the name Ntazina, which was a nick-name given to him by others, became accepted as his real name.

This testimony was given in the year 2000, when Mbazende was eleven. Since it was not possible to make it public then, I prudently decided to wait for the opportune time to publish this book. I was still in Rwanda, where freedom of speech does not exist, except in official documents presented to the International Community in order to win awards for *good governance*. Since I have recorded here not only testimony but also comments and analysis, there will be many things that will seem anachronistic. We need to understand them in today's light. Although the child's recounting of his story was not ongoing or sequential, we should respect his testimony. He recalls information as he remembers events, and I have decided to put them into chronological order.

In order to be a good Rwandan citizen, one must own a very nice vehicle—preferably a jeep—a nice villa—preferably in Nyarutarama or Remera village—and a cell phone for the management of one's affairs. Our companions are either Mayibobo like us, or bandits, or brothers, or prostitutes, who we call our sisters, when they are too drunk to make their way home from the nightclubs and join us in the streets. Consequently, I am a townsman, not because I was born in the capital city of Kigali, but because, here, I find all that I need to live. The garbage cans provide me with food. To fall asleep, I rely on drugs; I have to find a little bit of gasoline that I suck up from a soaked cloth or I need to drink a little specialized glue, as if I were a pair of shoes. Thanks to the glue—if I'm out of hemp—I sleep under the stars, like a baby, with not a care in the world. I don't have any blankets, and I have only one pair of pants and the short sleeved shirt I'm wearing. I would never have been able to get any sleep without these drugs. Head lice and fleas are my daily companions. They never leave me alone. They suck my blood mercilessly, but I understand them very well. Where can they find nourishment? They were created parasites to live on humans and animals. These lice are also an unimaginable asset to us. They keep us busy during lonely and sometimes terrifying nights, when it is raining or when the electricity goes out, as it often has lately in Kigali. I love these parasites because at least they have the human heart to accompany us wherever we go. They crawl all over our bodies and clothes, reminding us that we are forsaken and abandoned children. The bandits are our other inseparable companions, but we see them mostly at night. They send us to watch over their hit targets. Unfortunately, once they've robbed the place, they abandon us without paying us our commission. They are robbers even to that extent. The prostitutes of Kigali are also our nightly companions. Often, they'll spend the night with us in the streets or under the bridges of Kigali when they are dead drunk and not able to get home. We know how to select the prettiest and the youngest. It's those who are our age or a little older who attract us the most. Those as old as the sky don't interest us much, even if they pay us to allow them to cuddle up next to us for the night. I can put up with anything—days without eating, surviving the nights, the fatigue, and walking many kilometres.

One time, the police sent us, by force, to Gikongoro in big trucks. There, they wanted us to live a life controlled by the rhythm of drums and whistles like the soldiers or recruits did. I didn't like this lifestyle where you had to eat when you weren't hungry and sleep when you weren't tired or drugged, sleep for the sheer pleasure of sleeping. After three days, I was back in Kigali with most of my buddies. It was the same scenario when the police drove us out of the country to the island of Iwawa, situated in Lake Kivu far from Kigali. I was back in Kigali in two weeks. I was afraid that I would have to relive the same scenario as beforehand in Zaire. Besides, we were not far from the country (Zaire) that took away all of my family including my dear cousin Kayirangwa. So I crossed over on foot, pursued by the compatriots. I hated living where one guy—"*umuginga ufata ibyemezo wenyine akagutegeka kuryama utabishaka*"—thinks for everyone. They considered us immature and crazy. They ignored the fact that we were very resourceful! I hated what they called Dormitory. The first night sleeping between sheets was funny, believe me! I'm used to sleeping on a cardboard box or rolled up in a bag. In no way could I sleep there, where the lice couldn't get in and where I couldn't look at the sky to count the stars and thank God for those shiny things.

Forgive me for being so long-winded in my presentation and allow me to present my younger brother—or my child, if you will, since he calls me Dad. I believe that he has reason to. I'm seven years older than he is, and he never knew our dad. It's too bad! My mom named him *Birame*. This name means (a survivor of so many evils that attacked him). This explanation does not come from me.

It came from my mother. Actually, before succumbing to savage gunfire, she explained everything to me. "Birame," she said, "means one who has miraculously survived. This name that I'm giving to your baby brother, my child, it carries with it my wish. I want him to have a life so that he will grow up and return to the land of our ancestors."

As she lay dying, before taking her last breath, she told me that I must always carry my little brother on my back, never in my arms or on my head. She insisted that I must not seek revenge, even in my adult years, because God does not love those who seek vengeance. I've always kept that thought in my mind. But, believe me or not, it is difficult to remain faithful to her wishes. What really happened? This is the story.

AN ARDUOUS ODYSSEY:
FROM KATALE TO WALIKARE

Before speaking of this "way of the cross", I just remembered something that will never be erased from my memory: the attack on the
refugee camp in Kibumba. We were living in that refugee camp
with all of my family, including many cousins with whom we had
lived in the camps for displaced persons, from the moment the RPA
had chased us from our villages and our homes in 1990. During
our exile in Zaire, we lived here in the camp at Kibumba. I could
see volcanoes overhead. I didn't like to look at them; they terrified
me. I knew that therein lived *"Akavumburamashyiga kavumbura*
abana banga kuryama ntacyo bariye" (those flame–spitting eaters of
children who cry in the night and refuse to go to bed when they
haven't had anything to eat) or so my mom used to tell me. These
children refused to go to sleep until the parents would find something they could chew on. To me, the volcanoes resembled gigantic
straw houses with roofs of manioc flour. *–Mbazende referred to the*
clouds hovering over them–

I clearly remember the day that the RPA besieged our camp and
seeing my father cry, my beloved father who always told me that a
man never cries! It was the first and only time I ever saw him cry.
He said that the camp was surrounded by soldiers. He was crying
at the thought of losing us, as he had lost other family members
in 1994 during the destruction of camps for those displaced by
war. His loved ones died at the hands of the same army, the RPA.
He didn't think that we had any chance of survival. He began an
inventory of all our relatives who had perished in warfare because
of this army's attack, launched from Uganda on October 1st 1994.
Mom also made an inventory of her family members who had died
during that war. Dad spoke of his little brother killed at Kinihira, a
"no man's land" or buffer zone between the positions of these two

armies, RPA and RAF, from 1992 to 1994. They had been killed by rebels. Grandfather had been killed in the region of Kagitumba during the first moment of attacks in 1990. My grandmother died of diarrhea in Goma along with many more of our relatives. My two sisters had also been reported missing there.

After the destruction of this camp at Kibumba, we headed for the Katale refugee camp near Rutchuru, in north-eastern Kivu. We had to pass through the jungle of Rumangabo, where the Zairian military took shots at us. We spent only a short time at Katale because, a few days later, the same soldiers who destroyed Kibumba sacked this camp and destroyed it too. We abandoned it. It was during this second attack that I learned to differentiate the sound of various weapons, simple guns, machine guns, and mortars. I lived in the 4th Quarter. During the attack on Katale, my neighbour was killed by a bomb. Our *burende* (homes made with plastic tarps or sheets) were built side by side. The Zairian Contingents, the ZCCS soldiers, told us that the enemy had taken a detour, the road leading back to Rwanda from where they had come. But this was not true; they said this because they wanted to keep us calm. These soldiers had been abdicating and surrendering their positions on frontier lines to enemy soldiers. ZCCS had made a decision to leave us long before then. In other words, they had sold us to the enemy. During those days, I saw with my own eyes the UNZCCS soldiers packing up their belongings. After their departure, the assailants threw bombs and grenades on all sides of the camp and shots were fired all over. They killed the people who got caught, using anything they had, possibly knives or used hoes. Mortars, bomb launchers, were placed all over the camp especially at Biruma to the north of camp and at Karengera to the south as well as in the cafes and near the 3rd, 4th, 5th and 6th Quarters.

The camp had been established in an old park once inhabited by animals. But a long time before our coming, Ugandan refugees had tried to settle there. They had evacuated shortly thereafter because of areas emitting noxious volcanic gases called *mazouks*. We were in danger of asphyxiation by these gases that killed anything that had blood running through it, breathed, or came near it. Stories had been told how, in the past, Ugandan refugees died, cause unknown. Some chose, then, to go back home, thinking that it was maleficent spirits that had killed them. Nonetheless, Rwandans were forced to live there. For them, returning home would have meant being killed by the new government, the RPF, who defeated the RAF and were leading the country. Those soldiers killed Hutus at the borders of Rwanda and Uganda in 1990 and also destroyed camps for displaced refugees inside Rwanda. Refugees had no choice but to live in that camp despite the mazouks. To return to Rwanda would be suicide since it was well known that anyone who had ventured back, had been killed as soon as they had entered the country. The transit camp of Nkamira had the reputation of being the place where returning refugees were killed. But this was not the only way that we could be annihilated; even in the camp itself, if a refugee admitted to planning a return to our homeland in Rwanda, he could be killed by Interahamwe. So the refugees had to remain in the camp at all cost, while at the same time, finding a way to deal with those poisonous gases. Ingeniously, we found a miracle way to survive the effects of this gas. Whenever someone came into the mazouks zone that the refugees had carefully identified and isolated with barbed wire, he had to cut and bleed himself immediately to save his life. It is thanks to this ingenious strategy that the refugees resisted.

The entire camp of Katale consisted of sharp volcanic rock. One couldn't walk around without cutting the soles of his feet, so the refugees fabricated *rugabire* (sandals made from tires and nails). Sadly, it wasn't just anyone who could get a pair because the price was quite expensive for people without money. In spite of that, human imagination, misery, and an instinct to protect and to conserve helped them to transform this rocky territory into an oasis. If one were to compare the camp at Katale with the surrounding villages of Rutchuru, the area in which the camp was established, the difference would be the same as that between a big city and a shantytown in the outskirts. It was nearly a city in the countryside. With those rocks, the refugees built impenetrable fences, walls for houses in tarps. The refugees managed to build extraordinary homes from plastic, tarps, and sticks. Their houses were comfortable homes even having balconies, *barza*, and gigantic fences on which we could read "Beware of dog". One could even find bars and several-storied hotels. "La Merveille" or "Chez Célé" is an example of hotels that lacked nothing. One could find everything in which to drown one's sorrows: beer—though not *Mützig*, liquors, brandies, and all kinds of *urwagwa* (a very popular local wine made from banana juice). They also had *butunda* (another kind of banana wine, but stronger, since it was made from a pure juice blend of bananas and sorghum).

I liked to go the Second Quarter, below the football field to get *imbetezi* (the residue from *butunda*). Once extracted, this residue could be used to feed the poultry, which had become plentiful in the camp. When mom diluted it with water, we had a drink that tasted like *urwagwa*, and I loved it—don't be surprised because in Rwanda even children share drink with their parents. At the Katale camp we also found skewers of fish, goat, and grilled chicken or beef. Those who still had money, or those who had found a job at the camp, could treat themselves well. There was also entertainment to distract people: at community centres, concerts were held, with traditional dances, drums, and ballets such as *"Indangamuco z'amahoro"* from the NGO called OXFAM. These community centres served also as schools for refugee children. There were hospitals, nutrition centres and dispensaries. In nearly every Quarter, there was a church and almost all faiths were represented. For example in the 6th Quarter, we had Saint Francis of Assisi Cathedral—without a bishop of course! Next door was a library supervised by Mr. Jean Pierre Godding but managed by seminarians. These seminarians were attending the Major Seminary in Rwanda, but when war broke out, they fled the country like other people and were living in the community in the 12th Quarter. They were devoted to pastoral care and tended to the poor and marginalized. They provided material assistance, distributing food and clothing that the Congregation of the Sisters of Charity gave them. All of these things made Katale a little city envied by the natives.

PARTIES THAT ENDED IN CRIES—On October 23, 1996, a festive air permeated the camp of Katale. Several couples had received the sacrament of marriage in Saint Francis of Assisi Cathedral in the 6th Quarter. Marriages had also been performed in several Protestant churches. Nothing of this *Eldorado* was spared from the bursting of bombs and the splintering of volcanic rock. The joy of the day and the happiness of the newly married couples were followed by crying, mourning, and separation.

ATTACK ON THE KATALE REFUGEE CAMP—The advent of the destruction of this camp had been preceded by several signs and incidences. The Government of Kigali in Rwanda, through its army, the RPA, had attacked certain refugee camps in the south such as Birava, Panzi, and Kibumba. No one had accused them of doing so or held them accountable. Instead, many of the NGO services had closed down and moved on to set up in Rwanda. A few months beforehand, the Zairian military, probably in complicity with the RPA, had launched an operation to repatriate all the refugees found in the city of Goma and around the camps of Kibumba and Mugunga by force. Neither the UNHCR nor the International Community—if it still existed!—condemned these violations against the integrity of the country of Zaire and of the domain under the protection of the UNHCR since the refugee camps were guarded by contingents of Zairian soldiers working for UNHCR.

Also, when the refugee camps in the north refused to submit to the procedure of census by branding with indelible ink, the UNHCR and NGOs made each child of refugee parents wear a bracelet engraved with all his identification: name, parents, municipality and original territory. Why would they have done this if they had no intention of dismantling the refugee camps? They knew that when the children were separated from their parents, either by death or by wandering off, they would possibly be recognized later by family members in Rwanda—if they were lucky enough to arrive there or to find their relatives alive and not in prison! Another reason is that the same government of Kigali had demanded that the UNHCR, through the Zairian government, arrest those who had been identified as intimidators. So several people, mostly former politicians and others responsible for the refugees, were arrested. One priest was arrested among them. Those arrested were driven to Kinshasa, the Zairian capital. As the camps were progressively destroyed by invaders from Rwanda in the South, and later from the North, everyone kept the matter quiet.

This silence—was it diplomacy or complicity? The objective of the destruction of the refugee camps was clearly to kill the refugees, was it not? Otherwise, how can one explain why they would pursue them beyond the Zaire-Congolese border, the Zaire-Angolan, Zaire–Central African, or the Zaire-Zambian! Where were the International watchdogs? Did these satellite superpowers, who usually put everything that goes on in the world under a micro-scope, go blind or have their vision blurred? Or did they become blind when it came to killing Rwandans both within their boundaries and outside of them? Planes were flying overhead during our adventure. Were they not equipped to figure out that we were not on a leisurely walk in this vast country of multiple rivers, dense jungles, and wild animals?

There are reasons to pose many questions about what happened to Rwandans from 1990 to now. In 1994, human beings were inhumanely massacred by other human beings and no one intervened. Maybe the killers had become so monstrous that no one wanted to risk their own life attacking these vultures that were so thirsty for innocent blood! A wrong doing such as this would qualify as a legitimate defence if, in reality, the killers had grown so monstrous! Otherwise, not wanting to come to the aid of someone who is waiting impatiently and powerlessly for your help would be considered lax, negligent, or downright bloodthirsty. In other respects, how can one party—already victimized and abandoned, alone and without help—be allowed to hurl themselves onto other innocents on the pretext that among them may be their former execution-ers. That fact would not be tolerable unless one wanted to allow the long-offended party to console itself by committing the same crimes once committed on them. In this case, they would have had to monitor that an equal number were killed. In the opposite case, one would be accused of not coming to the assistance of persons in mortal danger and that would place one in the second category as a Genocide perpetrator. In conformity with the current Penal Code of Rwanda, the sentence would be incarceration for life or half a lifetime spent doing community service—see the category of Genocide perpetrators!

THE TERRIBLE NIGHT
THE DESTRUCTION OF KATALE

At that time, it seemed peaceful; there had been no bombs heard for the past three days, and people were once again frequenting the Lubale market. Nevertheless, the camp of Katale was completely destroyed during the night. We made our way toward the basalt jungle, and we were strictly prohibited from lighting even a small candle. We didn't have any shoes though the lucky few wore *rugabire*.

That night was the beginning of a long and endless road of death and suffering throughout the entire country of Zaire. It was the beginning of a voyage without destination, and massacres as never before seen or recognized by the biggest countries such as The United State of America, the United Kingdom, France, European community—and perhaps Canada as well since it was the General Maurice Baril, a Canadian commander of the United Nations Forces, to intervene in Zaire where the Hutus were massacred. This General established his headquarters at Entebbe in Uganda, one of the countries involved in the massacres and didn't intervene.

On the night in question, especially before 9 pm everything seemed calm. I had fallen asleep quickly that night because I no longer heard the echoing of bombs or the crack of gunshots. But around 9 pm, my mother woke us up by pouring cold water on us. I could hear the crackling of tarps, caused by refugees fleeing the camp. My dad was not with us because he was on night watch duty, so Mom had us carry the supplies. My cousin carried a full pot of beans, and I carried a bottle of oil labelled "USA" because it had been made in the United States of America. Nearly everyone in the camp headed to site "Q" at the far end the 7th Quarter and, beyond there, to a jungle where the distribution of food supplies for persons formerly from Kigali and Ruhengeri took place. From there began a journey to Calvary as never before! When the night became dark and obscure, we entered into the jungle of death. Since the beginning of the war, the men had guarded the camp at night to ensure that no assailants infiltrated while we slept.

We were previously prohibited from going in the direction of Tongo. Equally and as strictly prohibited was the use of a torchlight or other incandescent object, for the killers would surely follow the light, catch us, and decimate all of us. To the north of this camp was the refugee camp of Kahindo, and we hoped that, in passing by the volcanoes and the jungle, we would connect with the camp at Mugunga. This path did not extend a very warm welcome to us. It was full of jagged volcanic rock that made holes in the soles of my feet. We penetrated the jungle with Mugunga as our destination. We had been forewarned to stay as far away as possible from Tongo. Even if we weren't always sure of our location due to the density of the jungle, we kept this warning in mind. In the meantime, the rich—in their cars and trucks—had headed toward Tongo on the prohibited route; it took them less than three hours to get to Tongo, but it took the luckiest of us two days, and weeks and weeks for others. Many people perished in this jungle. Much suffering lay ahead for us.

Before the attack on the camp we were afraid to enter the jungle because of possible enemy ambushes; there were also wild animals and very sharp volcanic rocks. Even in peaceful times, no one would willingly expose themselves to the risks here. Unfortunately, the attention of the enemy had been directed here.

In that jungle, night became too heavy and sleepiness came upon us, trying to slow down our pace. But we had to keep moving in order to get as far away as possible. Anyone who lagged behind was swiftly killed by the assailants who pursued us. We had to forget about eating and drinking. It would have taken a miracle to find water to drink—we had no Moses with us to strike the volcanic basalt so that drinking water would flow from it. We lacked water and so learned to eat *imifumba* (herbaceous grasses in the forest that children like to eat because of its succulent juice). Sadly, here they did not contain any water or juice because of the heat and the type of soil made from the volcanic rock.

The pot of cooked beans that my cousin was carrying had already been spilled during the night when she slipped on some volcanic rock. No one had eaten yet and the jungle provided nothing but trees, not even enough of them to offer shade or edible fruit. As noon approached, things got worse. We had walked very far and perspired so much that we were exhausted and dehydrated. The sun, directly over-head, was scorching hot. Victims of hunger, thirst, and fatigue, no one felt able to take another step. Despite this, we tried to climb Bushoki. The climb up the volcano left more than one person defenceless. Not a tree, no vegetation whatsoever, was to be found on this volcano. It was nothing but pebbles and one could say that the sun was totally focused on it. We observed the comings and goings of adventurous refugees. We would climb up the volcano only to slide right back down, tumbling into anyone in our path. No one had the strength to resist the fall. If someone toppled over like a felled tree, death ensued. Subsequently, we gathered up some courage, and we eventually arrived, exhausted, at the peak of the volcano only to fall down the other side like stones. We couldn't believe it!

THE HOUR OF AGONY: 3 PM—Near three in the afternoon, the worst of the worst happened. We desperately needed to find something to drink. Where? How? Some, who were more resourceful than others, slit the throat of a chicken they still had in their possession since fleeing the camp. The hope of plucking it, once we arrived in an area where there would be water, was dimmed. Instead of quenching their thirst, the chicken blood led to the death of those who drank it. Others who tried to drink peanut oil, soya oil, or corn oil died also. Something rubbery formed in their mouth and possibly right down to their stomach. When we tried to pull it out of their mouth, we couldn't. Anyone who tried to drink these oils died instantly. Other people started slashing their veins to drink their own blood. They died as well. Of what? I wouldn't know how to explain it.

Some chose to drink their own urine. In fact, I witnessed a scuffle between two angry men. One of them had just urinated into a glass and the other, hearing him do so, asked him to share a little to quench the thirst of his dying child. Perhaps he had already tried to produce some himself but couldn't. The one who had urinated replied crossly: *"Wanyaye izawe wa nyana y'imbwa, we!"* (Urinate yourself, son-of-a-bitch!). Others, in order to get a reprieve from the sun, dug holes big enough to shelter their entire body. They looked like graves! They would bury themselves, being careful to let only their head stick out, then they would cover themselves with leaves. Thus, they were reduced to the level of earthworms and other crawling creatures. It didn't matter, so long as a life was saved.

Others taught us how to suck on tree roots, for the root sap contained water and minerals. Of course, we had to learn to choose those trees that were not poisonous. Safe selection was not easy, and a good number of people died from eating toxic plants. Again, we escaped death. It was not the first time that death came for me and yet I was still alive. After resorting to this regime, we gained strength and we were able to advance, even though we did not always know where we were headed. We were only a few kilometres from leaving the jungle when it started raining. Every person opened his mouth as wide as possible, and happy were those who could open their mouths really wide! We decided to strip so that we could be totally refreshed by this welcome and beneficial rain. It didn't last very long—in truth, good things never last long enough.

We forced ourselves to cover as many kilometres as possible, in the hope that we would make it out of the evil jungle. Thankfully, it was not long before a clearing came into view and we were free of the place. Many Rwandans and Burundians had met their death in that jungle. We kept telling ourselves that we would soon arrive in Mugunga. In reality, we were far from there. We found ourselves in Tongo, the one place we had so carefully tried to avoid. We were still a long way from Mugunga, but at least we had water and food in Tongo.

It was on the second day that we became separated from my cousin, Kayirangwa. We were thirsty, my mother and I. Dad had not yet rejoined us. Mom sent Kayirangwa to fetch some water from somewhere. We didn't know for sure, but it was said that water could be found in the volcanoes. We never set eyes on Kayirangwa again. She had gone with a group of people. Some of them came back, without water, but with the sad news of her death. Kayirangwa had been killed with several other refugees who had been on their way to the volcano to find water. When they reached the top of the volcano—*Nyiragongo* or possible *Nyamuragira*—the killers were waiting for them. They had been stalking them, knowing where they would have to go to get a supply of water. What cruelty! It constituted premeditated murder. It was planned, was it not? It was the only place where water could be found. When my mother heard this sad news, she was furious. Armed with blind courage, she planned to rush up to where the water was and perhaps bury Kayirangwa. We were told that it was actually about 60 kilometres away.

In the meantime, father had just rejoined us and dissuaded mom from heading in that direction. It had become a field of death. We decided to change direction. We had been heading for Tongo without knowing it or intending to do so. On the way, a thirsty man grabbed my bottle of oil. He assumed it was water, drank some of it and died. Within seconds of drinking it, he began to vomit something that looked like rubber. When my dad tried to pull it out of his mouth, the man fell to the ground and died. No one had the strength to bury him. Who could dig up volcanic rock, considering how we were all suffering from thirst and dehydration? We continued on our road to perdition. Many parents decided to rid themselves of their children, especially those they had been carrying on their backs. The elderly reached out to any generous person for help. Frankly speaking, no one was interested in anyone else. I believe that many bodies still lie in rest there and that their souls cry out for vengeance. On whom?

MURIMBI, PLACE OF RESPITE—Murimbi is the village in Tongo that we came upon just beyond the jungle. There, we found a little of everything: bananas, taro, potatoes and a lot of beans. Some, at their arrival, believed that they were already saved. They no longer thought about RPF soldiers who had caused them to flee and wished them nothing else but death. There, we met other refugees from our former camp in Katale.

They had arrived earlier, some hanging on to the sides of cars and trucks and others on foot. This road was the shortcut to which we had been denied access. Fortunately, we were warmly welcomed. Some brought potatoes, sweet potatoes and beans; others brought meat that, sadly, we were not able to swallow. We had sores all over the inside of our mouths and down our throats. Swallowing anything was painful. Only after a day or so here, were we able to swallow anything.

Dr. Bonaventure continuously tended to us. One by one, we began to settle in and prepare our own meals. In the meantime, many who had abandoned their loved ones in the jungle, brought water, food and broth to them. God only knows how many of them came back alive. A good many lost their way again, others found themselves on a road already blocked off to them. During this time, we kept busy installing tarps and selecting a location for housing native Zairians. For some, leaving this place was unthinkable.

As we were enjoying food, banana wine, and sorghum beer—two traditional drinks shared by the Zairians from the region of Kivu and Burundians—the assailants were preparing for their ultimate assault. They had barricaded the road to anyone who was still in the jungle and they killed large numbers of them. One afternoon, we heard the crackling of a Kalashnikov in the distance, followed by the sound of bombs exploding. Every refugee who had a vehicle ran to start it, even though the road was too narrow and pretty much impassable. No one would let anyone pass. There was a bulldozer that had begun to back up and, even though it hadn't gone more than 100 meters, a big truck belonging to a self-centered shop-keeper dashed onto the road, slid sideways, and ended up blocking up the entire roadway. No vehicle could get by and so everyone had to walk, abandoning everything they cherished. It was a shame because a fortune was left behind. The buses transporting the injured were abandoned, as were the injured themselves. You can imagine what their fate was. All the vehicles in Katale, the supplies and medications were left behind, thanks to the enemy. I believe that these same vehicles were later used by the enemy to chase us wherever we went and to kill those who fell behind. Every material good stayed in Katale. It was regrettable because many had placed their hopes in their possessions. What a shame!

We took the road near Masisi Center, believing that we were heading for Mugunga. A group of assailants were waiting for us on this very road; they were hiding in the grasslands and pastures that are plentiful in this region. It was a question of running our legs off and not thinking of hunger, thirst, fatigue, or the cold that gnawed at our bones right through to the spinal cord. Our safety depended on how we ran the race. Woe to him who lagged behind! Woe to him who was only being dragged along by the others!

It was so very cold in Tongo, but no one complained. One pressing thought preoccupied our minds: how were we to survive this night? It was in these grasslands that we spent the night. We crowded together to give each other courage. Even though we were strictly warned not to make any noise, mothers called out to their lost children. Husbands, as well, called out to their wives. We slept under the stars, our bellies ravenous. Anyone who could prepare a little broth waited until morning to do so. Very early in the morning, we resumed our adventure, hoping to be the first to arrive and thereby the first to plunder—to help ourselves to the Zairian supplies.

It was around noon that we were attacked while we were preparing some food. Again, we abandoned everything, pots, as well as the food that we had been preparing, and we took flight. We were not aware that an ambush awaited us somewhere around a bend. It was very traumatic to have to step over the bodies of those who had passed before us. Our survival was tenuous, for we were so tortured by fatigue, sleep deprivation, and hunger. Since the path was very narrow, we had to walk in single file. The road had become impassable because the inhabitants of Murimbi no longer engaged in any *Salongo* (community service). Whoever wandered from the line was lost for good. We had to walk with the father of the family in front, followed by the children, who were tethered to his belt. The mother followed them or another family member. A friend might also be in the lead. We had instinctively adopted the strategy of mountain gorillas. That is the way they travel; the strong ones lead, the old and the young next, then the mothers, and lastly a group of young, strong gorillas to protect the rear. This was the strategy used now by a people in distress. What had life come to?

Military RPF soldiers had been stationed at the end of the road. Since we were walking one behind the other, the first one to go around the bend had his throat swiftly slashed with a knife and then his body was pushed into a pauper's grave that had been prepared especially for this purpose. The coup was so well executed that those following didn't notice what had transpired and kept going as though nothing was wrong. Father was walking in front of me; I followed, and my mother was behind me. Dad was struck down with one blow from a bayonet. This same bayonet passed just above my head, and I screamed as I ran in the opposite direction. Everyone ran away with me, screaming. The killers attacked us with grenades and bullets. A great many refugees perished that day. We blazed a different trail and spent the night in another place called Gicanga. It was a large grassland where, when night fell, we piled up on one another like rotten tomatoes.

No one had time to prepare any food, and anyone who wanted to light a fire would get a bullet or rocket in his pot. This is a day that I'll never forget. In spite of the fatigue from our long day, the hunger that gnawed at us, the obscurity of the night, no one could sleep. We were preparing ourselves for an eternal sleep—do I dare say it?—a gift reserved for each of us. Everyone was a candidate for death. Death journeyed with each one of us.

In fact, from about 6 pm to 7 pm mortars launched rockets that lit up the night. I will never forget how a soldier came up and pointed his machine gun at our heads while we were sleeping under a hillock in the grasslands. We couldn't pitch tents. I wasn't cold that night even though it's usually extremely cold in Masisi, especially when it rains.

The rain fell on us for nearly three hours. I was warmed by my own urine because I would wet myself every time I heard a bomb blast. Oh my God, I was so scared! It was during that night that I decided to become a soldier to avenge my father's death. However, a lack of opportunity caused this vocational dream to blur and to finally disappear. In the morning, we saw bodies strewn all along the route. We once again lined up, following each other like ants, on our way to Mugunga.

Later, we set up camp at Rukwi, a large prairie separated by two sections of roadway. When we got to Rukwi, we were able to prepare the taro and potatoes that the local population had donated to us. The local chief—as was the custom—gave us a cow to butcher and the meat became, evidently, the prize for the strongest. We spent nearly two weeks here before beginning the biggest, if not the deadliest, adventure yet.

Life at Rukwi seemed to have fallen back into routine. Men were getting organized for their small business ventures and had built restaurants that served only potatoes, bananas, sweet potatoes and beans prepared with palm oil. As for drinks, one could find *kasigisi* (banana beer), *kanyanga* (highly alcoholic ethanol), *ubushera* (sorghum beer without yeast), *umutobe* (banana juice), and *ikigage* (sorghum beer made with yeast). Those who still had money could procure meat because they could buy goats.

Personal hygiene was one of the most difficult challenges we had to face. There was not enough water for such a large population. We would have to go all the way to the bottom of the valley to get either running water or swamp water. There was no way to wash up. During the entire time that I spent at Rukwi, I never took a bath due to this lack of water. My mother couldn't go down to the valley and then climb back up. It was too tiring for her. Another hindrance was that we had no toilets. Everyone made do as they wished. Some dug holes not more than a meter away. This hole would not be covered. Many people did not dig holes but would relieve themselves in the bushes. This is what my mother and I did. You can imagine what would happen when the rains came. There were flies everywhere! The stench was unpleasant to say the least. Diseases such as cholera and tubercular dysentery lay in wait for us. Luckily, we didn't stay there very long.

FATE'S END—For so long, we waited impatiently for the return to our native country. Everyone imagined the joy of homecoming. We were also curious to see how many people actually still lived in Rwanda because, in the camps, we had heard that the Hutu had been massacred and that whoever dared re-enter Rwanda had been wiped away from the world of the living, killed before even making it back home. They said that Nkamira was a gate to death. It was there that they killed everyone who came back, especially males. There was, evidently, some truth and some untruth in these communications. When war broke out at Bukavu, hope of going home waned little by little. When war reached the region of Goma, we told ourselves that the end of our fate was very near. There was no way we could ever dream of a peaceful return to our homeland, land of a thousand hills, a country once called *Swiss Africa, a country where life is beautiful,* as my mother loved to tell me. We did, nevertheless, keep a faint glimmer of hope. Besides, that was the reason for our journey toward Mugunga, for it is located near the Rwandan–Zairian border.

Rukwi was, in a sense, a resting place, one to which we would eventually return. Who would have thought that the camp at Mugunga would be destroyed? Its fall caused unprecedented confusion. Who would have believed it? While we were preparing to advance toward Mugunga, our transit camp on the way to Rwanda, we heard the terrible news of the destruction of this gigantic camp. Hope abandoned us forever. Some people from Katale had already arrived at Mugunga. These were lucky enough to pass through the jungle without choosing the wrong road and getting lost in Tongo like we did. They had just barely escaped the massacre occurring in the jungle of the volcanoes at the hands of the RPF soldiers. The others would be dead from exhaustion and lack of water because it took a very long time to find water to drink, even a drop! Besides these people from the Katale camp, other refugees, originally from Kibumba and Kahindo—the camps in the neighbourhood of Katale—had also gathered in the camp at Mugunga. The inhabitants of Kahindo had had the good luck of not getting lost and had found their way directly to Mugunga. They had had exceptionally good luck because a group of Rebels had hurried on ahead to await us in the volcanoes where we absolutely had to pass. Those who came back to us told us how they had escaped from these bloodthirsty soldiers of the RPF and their *Igihozo* (worn-down hoes) always ready to knock off our skulls. I call anyone who was fortunate enough to pass through there and not get killed, a survivor. The survivors of the Kibumba camp were also gathered at Mugunga waiting for an eventual return to Rwanda. Since we had arrived together, I assumed that we would return together, grouping all those from the north and a few brave ones from the south who had arrived at Mugunga at an earlier time. When we heard all these terrible accounts, we were tortured by grief and seized with fear.

At the very moment, as we were ruminating on our sorrow, it was our turn to be attacked. There was great panic and devastation. I will never forget a man named Mukingo with his megaphone that never left his side. Those who lived in the Katale camp surely remembered him and his megaphone. He urged the people to take the road leading to Rwanda, the only opening that the RPF soldiers who encircled us had left unblocked. Many, including mom, would have taken this road, had they not been informed of the massacres in the jungle and in the volcanoes, just before arriving in Mugunga. Those who had just escaped murder in the volcanoes of Sake and Mushaki had witnessed these things. Paralysed with fear, mom, who lagged behind the crowd, headed in the direction of Masisi. We wanted to get as far away as possible. Fleeing was our only chance for safety. We were encouraged by this hope. How many kilometres away were we from Kisangani? In all, several thousand to cross the dense, virgin jungle of Masisi and then to traverse the streams that fed the Zaire River. It's a long saga. An adventure was beginning. We ran across the large grassland of Masisi to finally find ourselves once again in the gigantic jungle that emerges at Walikare. There are many details that are important to mention here.

When we left Rukwi, we headed for Masisi Center. Since mom and I were too tired to keep up to the pace, she chose to walk behind the others. The advantage was in detecting dangerous areas and being able to avoid them. The drawback was the risk of not

.ough food because, whenever the refugees passed, they
..d anything that was edible. Another disadvantage was the
.litude of being apart from the others. It's like the African prov-
erbs says, "The antelope that wanders away from the herd becomes
gravy for hunters."

And so, one day, as we were approaching Masisi Center, we
arrived at an abandoned centre for refugees who were sick, old or
infirm. We decided to spend the night so that we could prepare
something to eat. There was water, as well as food, that had been
left behind by fleeing refugees. I don't know where my mother got
the idea to spend the night in the banana plantation instead of in
the primary school classrooms like the other refuges did. And what
we heard all night was the wailing and cries of misery from the
refugees who had spent the night in the classrooms. Very early in
the morning, we got up to leave and found they had all been killed.
They had been split in two or hacked into several pieces, killed with
their arms and legs bound behind their backs. It was the first time
I saw a naked adult and women split in two upwards from their
genitals. The following nights would be very long for me. I swear to
you that I only found sleep a whole month later in the jungle, where
mom and I were alone and the mutilated bodies of the refugees
were far behind us.

But, before arriving in this jungle, which holds a very painful
memory for me because here I lost my mom, let's get back to
another event, the after effects of which remain in my heart. To be
honest, what I experienced there made me insensitive to everything.

I fell ill and my fatigued mother decided to spend almost a week
where we were. One of the villagers hid us. Before allowing us to
stay, the arrangement was made that we would spend the night
among the cattle on his farm and during the day, we would hide
in the brush. This arrangement was high risk in itself since the RPF
soldiers could have come to take the cattle and found us, but we had
no choice but to stay at that farm. We had no shelter, none of any
kind. And of course, it rained on us. The sun beat down on us too. It
wasn't a big deal because we could endure fatigue, hunger, rain, and
sun. Anything is possible for someone running from death. The one

thing that we could not endure was having to stay three meters away from a paupers' grave, where soldiers, in denims and carrying guns, came to throw the refugee corpses. Also, the odour coming from there was, to say the least, very unpleasant. I always saw the executioners come around 6 am and then again at 6 or 7 in the evening to throw in the bodies. We could not leave our spot before they arrived to dispose of the corpses; otherwise, we could have met them and been killed once they found us and thus be numbered among them. In the morning, we would get up at 5 am to be sure to arrive before them. Our life there was one big torture. Believe me. You may ask yourself why we were condemned to live this way. It was so that we wouldn't leave any trail to attract the killers, we had to walk on the paths that they had already made. This made it difficult for them to imagine that anyone else could have passed by there. We had to spend the nights with the cattle because the soldiers went from house to house searching for refugees who might have been welcomed there. This would be a terrible situation because both the lodger and the owner would be killed. In order to not put our host in danger, we had to live on his farm where he sent us food and milk. He rendered us a huge service. May God reward him! Sadly, he was killed in spite of his generosity. The soldiers called a meeting for all the men in the locality. Everyone who showed up was killed. That's how the person who put us up was killed. They burned his house and ate his cattle. He belongs on my list of martyrs. God will avenge their blood. I firmly believe this.

We abandoned our hideout and distanced ourselves from this place after the assassination of our benefactor, the destruction of his home followed by the massacre of his entire family and anyone who happened to be an eyewitness to these murders. In reality, the danger that we wanted to avoid was pursuing us. We had to catch up to the refugees as quickly as possible because there, at least, we could provide mutual comfort to each other. There was also a better chance of escaping death as part of a large group. That is how we came to pass through one grassland after another, guided by local residents who, as is the custom, extended a sympathetic welcome to us. They gave us everything: food, sorghum beer, and firewood. I remember receiving a pair of pants and a knitted sweater to replace the tattered one that I was wearing. Mom had the benefit of a gift of two new loincloths and an *ingobyi* (what mothers use to carry children on their backs). I have kept it somewhere. I just couldn't throw it away. It's a legacy from my poor, dear mother. Every time I look at it, I remember the ignominious death of my father, my mother, and my cousin.

Another event still engraved in my memory is crossing the Nyabarongo (the biggest river in Rwanda). In order to cross it, those who had gone ahead of us had placed a very tall tree across the waters and, one meter above the tree, a rope stretched taut. Fear mustn't prevent anyone from crossing. Another problem came up for my mother; she had to hold me by the hand while her other hand held the little bag containing a pot, the two loincloths and the ingobyi. What did she do? She asked me to take hold of the rope, then close my eyes, and walk behind her while holding on to a loincloth. Since I had more confidence in her—taking into account the way she always treated me tenderly and hadn't abandoned me like a good number of women who were afraid to watch their children die—I confidently followed her. When I got to the other side of the river and looked down at the water. I saw a lot of floating bodies with ropes on their arms. They had been bound for sure. We were so paralysed with fear that we couldn't even prepare a soup. We endured the hunger and continued our journey. After walking several kilometres, I realized that my mother was very tired. We still had not found any sign that the refugees had passed by. It made sense to backtrack. Mom said we definitely needed to rejoin the others to see if some goodhearted person would look out for me. These words meant nothing to me because I thought that I would live with my mother forever. She, on the other hand, realized that her health was weakening and that she was soon to give birth. When we got back to the river, after having recited *Ndakuramusta Mariya* (a Hail Mary), we crossed the river in the same way as before.

The plan was a success. After three hours of walking, we met two native people out in a field. They were locals from the village where the refugees had been massacred. As we spoke, we realized that they were scolding us. They said, "Why did you come back to get us killed? Why didn't you throw yourselves into the Rushoga? Didn't it have enough water to end your suffering?"

They gave us two cooked potatoes and I could see steam coming off them. We ate these sweet potatoes with sorghum beer. We were comforted by their presence. Mom suggested that I stay with them. I don't know why she was going to leave me there, maybe to save my life. Even if they accepted her proposition, I refused to stay with them. I was very attached to my mother. Maybe I was right to stay with her, considering the role I was to play later in helping my little brother to survive. Mom was worried as she said her goodbyes. To hear her speak, one would've thought she only had a few hours to live, which, as it turns out, was true.

I didn't understand any of it. And so, heaving a huge sigh of discouragement, she took me by the hand to continue our walk. On the way she asked me a lot of questions like: What would you do if I were to die? Do you know your father's name and my name? We are originally from what prefecture, what municipality, what sector? What is your grandfather's name? When she asked me what I would do if she died, I burst into tears.

She hugged me tightly, holding me to her heart whose thumping resembled drumbeats. She whispered into my ear these words that torment me to this day: "My child, I'm going to leave you; be brave; act like a man. The Blessed Virgin Mary will come to take my place." She hung a miraculous medal around my neck. She pointed out to me some men who had spotted us, but she pretended to not have seen them.

We climbed down hurriedly into the river. It stunk and had corpses floating in it. It wasn't very deep so we were able to cross it. But mom had to push aside the bodies so that we could pass. When we climbed up on the other shore, my mother vomited. One of the four men who were RPF soldiers came up and warned us in Kinyarwanda, our mother language, to leave this place immediately. He said, "*Nyamuneka mwavuye aha hantu ko abantu twahiciye ari benshi ko tudashaka kuhicira abandi.*" (Please leave this place.

We killed many people here; we don't want to add you to those we killed).

He gave my mother a pill. She swallowed it right away, washing it down with this same river water, again pushing aside the corpses. Kill or cure! The water was not as wicked as the men who threw the bodies into the river. Her vomiting stopped. Once we got to the roadway, we saw the three other soldiers still sitting there cleaning their guns. They told the one who had come to our aid to kill us. He refused. He said in Kinyarwanda that he had done enough killing. "We have killed many; we need to stop the killing this time."

With a hand gesture, the other soldier signalled us to approach. Our "guardian angel" soldier whispered to us to run quickly up the little hill directly in front of us. It was a place where the refugees had probably gathered before being massacred. Corpses still filled the prairie. We could have tripped over pots, bed mats and food reserves left behind by the refugees. The grasses brushed lightly against us. So did the corpses.

We also found bodies piled one on top of the other at the top of the hill. We didn't have time to move them to see if we recognized anyone. The stench of blood overtook us. We were choking and so discouraged that we barrelled down the other side too rapidly. Kibabi, the next centre, welcomed us like heroes. Everyone was surprised to see us emerge alive from the place reputedly named "Golgotha".

An inspiring group of curious onlookers gathered around us. It seemed like I was giving a media conference. The questions posed by a spokesman, well-known for his military tactics, simulated a press conference. I was personally uplifted by these people who brought us food and drinks. Imagine this—they even brought us meat and rice! They had offered us beer, Primus, but mom turned down this beverage because the alcohol content was too high for us. She preferred Orange Fanta, a sweet citrus drink. We stayed there only one day. It was very beneficial to us. Mom was able to rest and I, along with the other children of Kibabi, scouted out the area. It was then that I discovered another paupers' grave, even bigger than previous ones. Then, on a nearby hill, RPF soldiers were launching bombs.

I asked who these soldiers were. The children with me replied in Swahili, *"Ni Barwandais"* (Rwandan soldiers). I got scared. While I was trying to decide how to escape them, a Toyota pick-up without license plates stopped in front of us.

From inside the vehicle, the soldiers asked us if we could show them which road would take them to their military buddies. They ordered us to get into the vehicle. As I was doing so, one of the soldiers stared at me and realized that I was a refugee. He said: *"Uri impunzi wowe sha ntutubeshye."* (You're a refugee and don't try to lie to me).

I was trembling with fear as I nodded my head and right away I apologized—as if being a refugee had become a sin—saying, "Don't kill me; God will reward you."

Another one said to me, *"Wigira ubwoba, kadogo, ntitukwica, uzabara inkuru y'ibyabaye."* (Don't be afraid, kadogo; we won't kill you. You can tell us what you have lived through).

I couldn't believe my ears because I had seen a lot of corpses of children my age. As I got near them, fear overtook me again. My eyes nearly popped out of their sockets when another soldier said, *"Adui ule"* (That one is an enemy).

A thin-faced soldier holding a bayonet came toward me. I felt like David of the Bible facing Goliath, except, unfortunately, I didn't have a slingshot to split open his face and head like David did in his time. I felt like a grain of sand facing a gigantic mountain. I began to rub the medal around my neck and utter this prayer, "Marie, Immaculate Virgin, protect me." I repeated this several times.

Another soldier came to give me a can of food. The one who stood before me, to terrify me, grabbed the can from his hand, threw it far away and yelled at him, "You're feeding the enemy! We need to beat him to death instead."

The one who had approached, without saying a word, left only to return later with another soldier they called Afandi. This one was my savior. Upon arriving, he told my tormentor: "Put that bayonet into your sheath. Get back to the others immediately. This child should not be put to death. He will represent the ethnic Hutu that we must decimate!"

Afandi—that was his name—took me by the hand and led me to their vehicle. He gently helped me to get in. After having fed me with canned goods, he began to question me, to test me to find out who I really was. My physical characteristics did not resemble the Hutu. As a matter of fact, my mother was Tutsi and my father Hutu. My facial features resembled my mother. It was due to my father's protection that mom had been spared during the Genocide. Even in the camps, she hadn't the least problem, thanks always to dad. All of mom's family had been annihilated during the Genocide by the Hutu extremists and nearly all my entire father's family had been uprooted in October 1990, then again in 1992, and again 1995 by the RPF soldiers—the same troops who killed him in 1996, and the same ones who were pursuing us and threatening our lives. I was left with no family. When I returned to my country, I had to become Mayibobo. They're my new family. Afandi asked me these questions:

"I don't think that you are Hutu. Are you a refugee?"

"No. I am Zairian." I said, "My family has lived here for a long time."

"Why are you trembling with fear? Because of all the corpses you've seen? Did you see who was killing them?"

"No," I said, "I was always in hiding."

"Are you not, then, a refugee?"

"My family has been in exile for a long time." With these words he took me again by the hand. He helped me to get out of the pickup. He accompanied me back to the other soldiers. He told them in Swahili, *"Petit huu ni wetu."* (This boy is our blood)— meaning that I was Tutsi.

Another soldier came to interrogate me. "What is your father's name?"

"My dad's name is Rugaravu," I said, "But he is dead."

"How did he die?"

At the embarrassing question, I stood gaping, open-mouthed. I thought that if I told the whole truth, they would kill me on the spot, because some guys among those soldiers were saying loudly: "Let us kill him. The infant of a serpent is a serpent too. Sooner or later he will seek revenge on us or our children."

But the Afandi continued his interrogation:

"Where does your mother live?"

"She's no longer alive," I said.

"Well then, we'll take you with us. We'll protect you and drive you to Rwanda, your native country."

With these words, I glanced away and in the blink of an eye, I saw, once again, the corpses left in our pathways. I realized that I was to become like them very soon. I was so traumatized that I started galloping at full speed away from them. A soldier tried to grab me. Afandi told him to let me be. "We mustn't traumatize him any more," he told him.

I told myself that if they took me back with them, without a doubt, they would kill me in the same way they had killed all the others. I could never forget how they killed my father, my grandfather and the others, so I ran as fast as I could away from them. When I got back to the village houses, I found my mom worried sick about me. When she saw me, she cried out: "Oh! praise the Lord. You're alive!" She hugged me tightly against her and asked me where I had been and what I had seen.

I told her everything, not omitting any details. She told me: "You, too, were to be killed. You must never leave your mother's side, my child. I love you very much, and I don't want to lose you as I lost your father and your cousin most recently. You were right to think of coming back to me because those people do not love." She added that shedding blood was the only thing that mattered to those soldiers. She continued on: "I am of their blood but they are going too far with their slaughters. Let's leave this place. They may follow you. I know them. They could come back to find us."

I calmed my dear mother by telling her that I knew exactly their location and that I would show her a safe road to avoid meeting up with them. I believed that I had all the information I needed. We took a shortcut that would allow us to rejoin the other refugees more quickly and to avoid getting killed. We arrived at Katoyi. It was an ex-refugee camp, now destroyed by these soldiers. This became evident by the bodies lying on the road and everything chaotically abandoned.

Near Katoyi-Center we could smell hemp burning. We sensed danger. To avoid it, we passed through a stagnant marsh with reeds on both sides. It was dusk and I wondered if we were going to spend the night in these waters. We noticed something far off that sparkled. Mom said we had good luck and that we were approaching an inhabited area. Although, we hesitated to approach it because, once again, it could be Death in the form of an enemy soldier's body who was awaiting us. But, since we had no other choice, no other place to go, we followed this light which led us to a house on top of a hill. It was the home of the former King of this region. Hospitality was quickly extended to us; food and hot water were served. We spent the night with the King. What a King! Frankly, he didn't look like a King. Nothing distinguished him from his subjects, except that he was goodhearted and well respected, despite his minimal attractiveness. He wore pants and a shirt like everyone else. Nothing about his appearance would have indicated his royal status.

Very early in the morning, the Courtiers accompanied us. They gave us portions of manioc and sorghum flour to make broth. Naturally, there was no sugar in the kingdom, not even for the King. They showed us another shortcut so that we could avoid going up and down the hills. We penetrated a dense jungle. We spent the nights and the next days alone. We were happy to have bananas and sugar cane to eat. We were afraid to even light a fire in this solitary jungle inhabited by wild animals, yes, real animals as well as the human beings who acted like them.

After two days of walking, we caught up to some men, who were, unfortunately, RPF soldiers—those wild animals in human bodies! We had a feeling that we were going to be victims of their wickedness even if they spoke nicely to us and said that they wouldn't kill refugees. They would tell us that it was the Habyarimana soldiers doing the killing. They always spoke in our language and, in the end, they left us. I said to myself that it would be with these sweet words that they come to kill their victims, like a cat plays with a mouse before killing it. Surprisingly, they didn't kill us.

We left them behind us. Meanwhile, my mother was tired from the trip and the pregnancy, and of course she was afraid. I was dragging my feet behind her, crying and refusing to take another step. The jagged rock, the trees, and brambles had made holes in my feet. I wanted my mother to carry me on her back like a baby. Of course, she wasn't able to. Death would have been welcomed by me that day since I was so tired!

After we had left the soldiers, we ran as fast as we could to ensure that a significant distance separated us from them. Eventually, mom had to slow down to my pace, and the assailants behind, of course, caught up to us. Thankfully, mom came up with the idea to quickly hide in a nearby hole, possibly a cavern or a foxhole. Anyway, it was as big as a house and it was full of ants. Believe me, they were not kindly ants. To prevent my cries from being heard because of the ant bites, mom put a pair of socks in my mouth. My dad had worn these socks prior to his death, his murder at Gicanga. They smelled badly because they hadn't been washed but I didn't howl for I knew that we couldn't make a sound because our enemy was tailing us and death was very near.

In reality, our enemy was very close by. What good luck we had that day! The soldiers, dressed in black jeans and rubber boots, were not those we had left behind us but probably another troop. They came to hide two wooden cases in the very same hole that we were in, and just left them there. It was in that way that the RPF's soldiers were provided with munitions. They worked in teams: some would infiltrate the groups of refugees and walk along with them. Others would follow to kill any who fell behind because of fatigue, hunger or injuries, and still others were spread out in the jungle like stalking predators.

Unaware of the content of those wooden boxes, I would have jumped on them if mom hadn't stopped me by tying my arms together with cloths. She told me that perhaps they were grenades or bombs. I had no idea what a bomb looked like. From my mom's explanation, I figured they were probably bombs and I had a burning desire to open the case, grab some of them and throw them at the soldiers to avenge the death of my father and cousin Kayirangwa.

Fortunately, my mother kept her eye on me and prevented me from doing so. Also, I hadn't realized that to throw a bomb on someone, a launcher is needed. I thought that I could throw a bomb in the same way that I threw stones to kill birds. I was of course wrong. As soon as these soldiers left, we got out of our hiding place, distancing ourselves as much as possible from the road taken by those refugees, and heading in the opposite direction. We were fleeing death without realizing that he moved with us or behind us, dressed in denim pants, plastic boots and kepis and speaking Kinyarwanda, Swahili, or English. These soldiers were so cruel! Instead of attacking the people who had the strength to run away, they usually started with the weak who lagged behind. This would include pregnant mothers, children separated from their parents, the old and the sick. As they say in our language: *"Ukubita imbeba ntababarira ihaka."* (One who kills mice will not take pity on one that is pregnant). Once the soldiers had gone, we got out of our hiding place to continue our journey behind them. The voyage was long and unbearable, especially because it was the rainy season. Since there were a lot of people travelling this road, sometimes to the extent of bumping into each other, the road became very slippery, so much so that people were falling on top of each other causing injuries, fractures and sprains.

Many children were separated from their parents. I was lucky to be with my mom. I was so frightened that I clung to my mother. We found ourselves on a slope that was very slippery because of the mud. It had rained abundantly during this season. It was difficult for mom to go down the slope—I wanted to let go of her hand so I could easily "ski" down the muddy slope— otherwise, she would not have prevented me from doing so. It was fun. I didn't know that she would be leaving me shortly.

We arrived at the Tebero Center, happy to be rejoining the others at Walikare. According to the natives who were tired of seeing us, cookies were being distributed by the French and the UNHRC staff members. Instead of finding them, we heard a lot of gunfire. We found ourselves lying flat on the ground. The groans coming from my mother were getting louder and frightened me. Mom had fallen belly first to the ground. She couldn't get up. I couldn't lift her up and I was scared but just for a minute. I forget the date, but because it was raining a lot, it seemed more like April rather than December.

Before dying, Mom said, "Immaculate Conception, take care of my children because I am leaving. Be their mother, now."

It must have been December 8th, 1996 because Father X told me that the Feast of the Immaculate Conception falls on December 8th. That day I remember being so afraid when I heard my mom groaning. Suddenly, I heard a loud noise like a clap of thunder and we fell to the ground. As I lay in the mud, I heard my mom scream and breathe heavily. She was lying with her belly to the ground. I tried over and over to lift her. She was too heavy for me and her groans made me lose courage too. I started to cry.

Suddenly a woman in her seventies came out of nowhere—for sure from her hidden place in that jungle—crawling on her hands and knees toward us. It had been a long time since I had seen anyone around. After some time my mom said, "Ugh! I have delivered!"

I heard the cry of a new born baby, but I didn't know where it came from. Mom was all covered in blood and she showed me, with a wink, something covered in blood. I had no idea what it was. I was already disgusted with blood, having seen enough in my life. I wasn't even curious enough to ask what it was. The only obvious thing was that mom wasn't wearing any loincloth. I only understood it was a baby when this old, wise woman showed him to me after he had been washed up. Then, he was given back to my mother. She said to me, "Thank God, I have just given you a boy. He is nice you know! I am naming him Birame."

We knew that our assailants were not far from us because bullets and bombs exploded nearby. After having spoken to me about our past and how we were obliged to abandon our country that was, as she put it, "flowing with milk and honey," she explained the significance of this name. I watched the old lady slip away, running as fast as she could into the evil jungle. There was such an air of death, death that ruled like a skilled dictator. I wanted to run too, but my mother begged me incessantly to stay close to her. There was the explosion of bombs, alternating with the crackling of gunfire. I couldn't budge but at the same time I was trembling.

With the help of a cane that the old woman had left behind in her hurry to escape, my mom struggled to stand up even though she was staggering. She managed to bind the child onto my back. She begged me to never carry him in my arms or on my head—I couldn't have done so anyway! We hadn't taken ten steps when I saw blood gushing out of her head. Mom, lying helplessly on the ground managed to tell me, "This is it for me."

I hate war and any person who provokes it!

—At this point the child is silent for a few minutes.—

Um! I don't know where I went. Let's continue. Fear paralysed me, and I sat on the ground next to my dear mother, crying. My little brother was heavy on my back and I didn't know what to do about his crying. I thought about laying him down on the ground and going far away from my mother who looked like she was sleeping, but with her eyes open.

I had to move away from her for a minute, now that the child wasn't as heavy anymore. Otherwise, she would have hit me with her cane! I didn't have the strength to take the child off my back. I didn't even manage to untie the lambskin ingobyi in which I carried the baby. This must have taken place over a span of several hours. I told myself that when Mom would take the yoke of this baby brother off my back, I would distance myself from her so that I would never again have to carry this heavy child. At the same time though, I feared the shadowy jungle where no one could be seen.[2]

Other than the noise caused by bombs and gunfire, there was deadly silence. I thought that she would wake up to feed me. It had been a long time since she had given me any food. I was angry with her because she wouldn't wake up. I decided to abandon her there, to leave her alone. I took but a couple of steps then I came back and sat next to her. From that moment on, I began to nourish myself with garbage in the woods and whatever had been left behind by the refugees who had passed there before us. This was all that was available to me as nourishment for my little brother and myself.

---

2   — By all rights this child should have gone crazy: He witnessed a birth, saw his mother's nakedness, was imposed the responsibility, at 7 years old, of taking care of his infant brother and all this in conditions of violence and massacres.

From time to time, I had to supplement my diet with snails that I burned on camp fires left by fleeing refugees. My child had stopped crying. Maybe he didn't have any more strength! Maybe he didn't want to distress me with his crying or maybe he knew it was not a good time to cry.

Satiated with the garbage here, I set out to find some other people. Where were they? I knew nothing. I took the road that lay before me. Wherever the refugees had passed, they had thankfully left a trail behind them. I was hungry. But, what could I eat? To whom could I turn, now that I had left my mother? Who could reassure me that she really was dead? My leaving had been a rebellious act. I still harboured the thought that she would soon wake up and come after me or at least prevent me from leaving her side as she usually did. I ascertained that she didn't want to wake up and feed me as she always did. I lost a mother who loved me very much. Would she ever have done like other mothers and fathers who abandoned their children in the jungle or who voluntarily got rid of them by throwing them into the rivers? I don't think so. What a painful memory! What a story! What a life! I can still hear the screams of the children abandoned in the jungles, calling out to their parents. I can only imagine how they were chewed up by the wild animals who never took their eyes off us.

From time to time, we would get into difficult situations, such as the day we *twaragiye imbogo* (guarded the buffalo) as we say in our street jargon, meaning a day without putting anything into our mouth, a day without food. O my! Sometimes this went on for several days! But it didn't matter to my little brother and me, for we were able to endure fatigue and hunger. We spent a lot of time without food. We were trained by the jungle. We had enough of that experience. From the time of my mother's death, I learned to gather up any food left along the wayside and I could make gruel in a tomato sauce can that I was able to carry. I was so weak and tired of the jungle and the long endless journey. Even though my stomach was racked by hunger and my feet paralysed, I was blinded by the fear of dying. Death was always an imminent possibility. My son never got down from my back, never! Even to feed him. I would bring my hand up to his mouth which automatically opened wide like a crocodile approaching its prey. He managed to get the food into his mouth. It was like feeding a baby bird. To make the gruel, I used a sort of blowtorch that I had made. This is how I managed to keep him alive. I'm very proud of myself. I'm a good mom!

I beg you not to cry. I didn't cry either. I was always the last to leave, and I took advantage of the fire left by fleeing refugees to cook my snails. I knew how to hide myself and avoid being seen. My size was an asset. Thankfully, my little brother—more like my child—didn't cry anymore either. He had no tears left. I think they dried up soon after losing his mother. When one is no longer with their mother, there's no reason to joke around. Goodbye to whimpers and children's games! This world is like a jungle where one has to take care of oneself, otherwise die. Since the departure from my mom's side, no one came to our aid. We learned to be resourceful, to take care of ourselves.

For example, in the jungle, instead of helping us, our compatriot RPF soldiers fired at us and, by chance, the bombs went over our heads. Thank goodness for my small stature! As far as the noise, oh my! It was terrible at first, but once we became accustomed, I swear it was beautiful music! For nutritional variety, I would gather bananas and ripe fruit along the way. Even though they were rotten, these bananas, left behind by fleeing refugees, saved our lives. There was nothing we could do about it. The child gained more and more weight as I lost weight. When I was with my mom, I was afraid of everything and nothing. But now I had said goodbye to panic.

On my journey, I had seen many abominable things, such as men who had been murdered and women hacked into pieces. Some of them still carried their babies inside of them. Oh, it was horrible! Oh, the wickedness of men is unimaginable! What they do is evil and barbaric! I saw corpses of children my age, some older, and again others younger than myself. My fear disappeared for good when I met, in the woods, an older girl from whom the Rebels had carved roasts of meat from her right thigh near her genitalia. Motionless, she lay in the bloodbath. I saw other wounds on her chest. She didn't have a shred of clothes on. While I was looking at her, she wiggled her fingers to tell me that she was not yet dead. She was still breathing. I approached her and gave her a banana that she couldn't manage to eat. I felt so sorry for her that I wanted to stay with her so we could die together. Again I heard the noise of handguns. Sadly, I left her there, after having covered her privates with foliage from the trees, in the place of underwear. I met many other amputees who had lost at least one limb. Some had no arms or legs. What I hated the most was the fact that they undressed the bodies so that they could plunder their clothing. Many bodies had suffered from intestinal worms and had large distended stomachs. But many of the bodies were already corpses. It was horrible to see those bodies, believe me.

All along this road, I had trouble finding water to drink. There were a great many streams but they were all full of bodies, so much so that, at a certain point, I had to resolve myself to drinking this water. What else could I do? Die of thirst along with the hunger that gnawed at my stomach? A lot of fat covered these streams and though I tried to expose the water beneath, as you might guess, I was not able to, and so I drank of this "water à la human fat!" I presume that other refugees did as well. For sure, some would have carried disinfectants for water, but that would be only a small handful.

Since that time, I learned to never again feel nausea or fear. And I still don't. That's why, when the police pick us up to take us somewhere, when I'm hanging on the side of a truck, I'm not afraid to make a dangerous jump to find myself safe and sound on the ground like a real commando.

My little brother knows how to do it too. I coach him all the time because he is my son. I want him to become a Rambo. We're always first in the garbage trucks ferreting out some bread, fries, and empty cans. Even if they're empty, they still smell like sardines when we put hot water in them. It's not bad. The other Mayibobo have nicknamed me *Ntwari* (brave) because I'm not afraid of anything or anyone. Fear and the word impossible were buried together near Tebero, where I lost my dear mother and became a mother myself to my little brother.

Once I stole a Motorola Radio from an Afandi, a Colonel, while he had five soldiers escorting him. I wanted to prove my valour. It's too bad the soldiers don't know what they're doing and have no confidence in those they are guarding. I don't want to be a soldier anymore. Otherwise, whoever was to be my bodyguard would have to be brave like Rambo, not just an adventurer. Any Mayibobo who manages to grab sugarcane must give me my share. When the trucks stop at red lights, I send brave Mayibobo to unload them. I know how to choose the targets and my operations never fail. Whoever helps himself to the *Daihatsu* loaded with potatoes from Ruhengeri fills his stock in front of me. I am the only one who distributes the goods according to each one's bravery. Now, that is justice, right!

All the Mayibobo have great confidence in me. I am proud that you know how I have learned to be responsible. I applaud myself for living life freely, yet responsibly. That is what made me capable of fending for myself today. As a matter of fact, I'm not ashamed of scrounging around in garbage cans for food. I, who have even eaten snails, what wouldn't I eat? I am an expert in the execution of a robbery. My plan never fails. How could I fail, I who managed after my mother's departure into eternity, to pass through a line of soldiers shooting at us. Night or day, rain or shine, never have my operations failed. I am not like those soldiers who always lose the battle. Failure? Intolerable! In the foster families, where I was forced to live, I became the vice-head of the family, directly under the father. I knew how to organize the children in the family in a rebellion against the mother who wanted to supervise our every move, as if we were not capable of taking care of ourselves. I can't live for very long in a group that doesn't recognize my leadership qualities. I don't take orders from others. I like the title *Kazagwa* or *Kaddafi* (gang).

My operations succeed because of my strategy to attack as quickly as possible without wasting time deliberating what should be done. I decide on the spot, and I don't want anyone giving me advice or contradicting me. Negotiation is the tool of the weak. Their plight is always failure. I hate failure. I always tell my guys that if we were to set the same quantity of straw in two locations, at an equal distance away from the donkey, the donkey would die from indecision. A donkey is too stupid to make a quick decision. I will never act like this animal! There are generals who spend a lot of time scrupulously preparing their attack. They are caught off guard and the attack fails. Meticulous preparation doesn't serve any purpose.

I am loved by all the Mayibobo of Kigali. They understand that I have to organize them to find food for all of us. And I always succeed in a variety of ways. I will go to places where even the bandits are afraid to go. My Mayibobo and I are the ones they send to case an area or to find out where the night guards are stationed. They know my signals: if I point to the ground, they know I am telling them to lie down. If I raise my hand high, they know that I am asking them to stop without making the slightest noise. If I say "zig" it means to scatter in all directions, running in a zigzag pattern. Those who are pursuing us don't know what to do. When they go to grab one, they see another running nearby. In the meantime, they are indecisive and already I have been successful in swiping what I came for. When I give a little whistle, everyone runs straight ahead in the direction he came from without turning around. They know our meeting place.

This is how we make away with handbags from distracted women. One time, I saw a beautiful lady getting out of a Mercedes Benz. I approached her and tapped her right on the buttocks. When she turned around to push me away, I gave her a big kiss that she immediately started wiping off her lips. In the meantime, my commandos had already seized her handbag. Then I whistled to start the game. That day, we gained a considerable fortune: a cell phone, many 5000 FR bills as well as many dollars. We found a passport in her handbag, but I ordered my boys to disguise themselves and return it to the car, which they succeeded in doing. I know at what time most of the watchmen fall asleep; at around 3 am, everyone is snoring. It's at that time that I steal their weapons such as machetes, swords, or bows to demonstrate my strength and power to my footmen, the frightened Mayibobo. The next day I sell them for money. I am not afraid of anything, *narikukiye,* for I too am a strong man of Kigali. We are the only two in this country.

THE DOWNFALL OF HUMANITY—
THE DESTRUCTION OF TINGI-TINGI

INHUMAN LIFE IN TINGI-TINGI CAMP—I am also an expert in military tactics. Did you know that? I have had a lot of experience. Do you know how I crossed the bridge over the Oso River? Truly a commando operation, I swear! When they were destroying the bridge, I was not far from it. Like a qualified journalist, I was observing difficult combat between the Zairian soldiers and the rebels. All the same, I was scared to death that day. As a matter of fact, we were quite accustomed to PUMA attacks, by those Zairian helicopters piloted by white men, the mercenaries. Suddenly, we were being attacked by two planes whose noise ripped branches from the trees and whose bright lights blinded and confused us. I was still in the Rebel camp on the other side of the river. I saw people dying like flies. Their bones were lifted up into the air. I defecated in my denim shorts with every bombing. It was horribly terrifying. The Zairian soldiers, profiting from the chaos in the rebel camp, destroyed the bridge. They believed this would prevent the rebels from crossing to the other side. They were wrong. I took advantage of their retreat to grab the boxes of cookies and the canned goods left behind during their catastrophic flight. Unfortunately, I could take only two boxes of cookies and two cans of sardines. These were very difficult to open. When I arrived at the refugee camp of Amisi, I got some help from one of the refugees and subsequently shared with him. I had to wait for the bridge, destroyed by the soldiers who had fled beforehand, to be repaired. Thanks to my size, I could pass, without being seen or recognized, through the ranks of soldiers lined up here and there.

In the morning, I was at the Amisi camp ready to watch a fight. What did we see? It was an endless column of men wearing their *kepi*, khaki green pants, and morning coats. They were marching six by six. Among them, one had a radio transmitter and the others carried guns. One carried a *kibariga* (a gun with a boom box that made a lot of noise). I had retreated only a few metres from the camp. Since I wasn't feeling well, I didn't want to live among the refugees. I had not washed up since leaving my mother's side. Well, once, but without soap and in water where human bodies floated. Also, I dreaded running out of food, which was a reasonable possibility, considering the large number of refugees living in the camp. I wouldn't even be able to eat snails, the hearty meal to which I had grown accustomed. I wanted to be free because some refugees were taking the liberty of hitting others. Some made themselves boss over the other refugees, giving themselves power to decide life or death. It really was awful. "There's no animal worse than man himself," as my mother would say, before she gave up her soul.

The rebels launched a surprise attack, a far-reaching one. To save themselves, Zairian soldiers ran as fast as their legs could carry them. They left behind their stock of weapons and their combat gear. The attack lasted all morning. As afternoon neared, I witnessed a fierce counter-attack. The Zairian soldiers—or rather Zairian soldiers with Ex-Rwandan army Forces, RAF, recognizable by their Lingala accent—came back determined to fight. They were singing in Lingala to give each other courage. *"Mosala oyo, oza mosala te bandeko!"* (This work is not a hard work! Let us finish it).

In the meantime, the rebels had had the time to dig *indaki* (holes) for themselves and to get prepared. And so from the direction of Amisi, mortars began spewing bombs. Handguns and grenades exploded in the rebel camp. An Afandi with a Motorola told the rebels in Swahili *"Hamuweze kurudi nyuma."* (Do not retreat under any circumstances) "Let's move in," he said, "Let's attack. Let's break their resistance. Well then, let's go!" When he yelled, "FIRE!" the mortars began to launch bombs at the Zairian soldiers. I saw a good number of them fall.

Suddenly, two PUMA helicopters from the ZAF began bombarding the ranks of rebels who were trying unsuccessfully to fire back. The worst was yet to come. Actually, while the rebels were trying to evacuate their dead and wounded, two fighter planes, ingenuous as snow, fired at them again.

The rebels were saying *"Atensheni, teyikingi kava, Mayiraji Français..."* (Pay attention! take cover, French Mirage...) After this bombardment, it was every man for himself as the rebels retreated. The ZAF, taking advantage of their retreat, recovered the weapons and rations that they had abandoned. They also took the uniforms off the dead bodies of RPF soldiers, the radios, guns and the Motorola. I saw these last two terrible planes circle back. They began dropping bombs on the soldiers who had not been hit but were brandishing high their flags to prove that they were not rebels. The planes left again. The refugees seized this moment to raid the food and medicinal supplies of the HCR.

I came out of my hiding place and into the camp. There was widespread panic in the Amisi refugee camp. I decided to head out to the camp at Tingi-Tingi several kilometres to the north. At nightfall, I took my child and began walking in the direction of Tingi-Tingi which harboured a large number of refugees from North and South Kivu. After three days and three nights, I arrived at Tingi-Tingi, but, in the meantime, refugees from the Amisi Camp had already out-distanced me. They were probably fleeing from other attacks whose echoing bombs I had heard far off.

Those of us from Amisi refugee camp were prevented from mixing with the other refugees of Tingi-Tingi. They feared any infiltration. People of this refugee camp had suffered a lot. Life at camp was very difficult because hunger raged and people were very tired. Life in Tingi-Tingi Hutu refugee camp was inhuman. It was so difficult that even the most respected ex-dignitaries in Rwanda would line up with the children to get broth from UNICEF or Food For The Hungry (FHI) that were, at that period of time, giving food to the children without parents. To look like children, they would slouch down, though it was rare that they were not found out and beaten by the guardians. Another worrisome phenomenon was to see them chasing lice in their clothing and undergarments, even though they would try to hide themselves from watchful eyes.

December and January were unforgettable months for those of us who were in the camp. Some were starving and so thin that when an airplane took off or landed, many had to lie on their bellies and cling to the ground so that they wouldn't be carried away by the draft created by the plane. It was a common occurrence, inside the camp, to see adults crawling around on their hands and knees like babies learning to walk. This is the only way that they could make it over small mounds because they were so weak. It was very distressing to witness adults, thin as bones, unable to walk over uneven ground without having to sit and roll on their buttocks. It took a very long time before food was sent to these refugees. The NGOs and Caritas Internationalis had not yet begun to distribute food packages, potable water, and soap. This so called "distribution" finally came, but much later.

Refugees had to learn to eat anything. In fact, when we hear the testimony of refugees who crossed the jungle of Congo, we are shocked by what they ate during these turbulent periods. They had no choice but to eat whatever they found along the way which is unthinkable for a Rwandan or Burundian. As soon as they exited the jungle of mabungu, there was no more taro and finding food was very difficult. This bad situation started when we arrived in Walikare, where there were no more *mabungu* and its inhabitants were not kind to us. Anyone who would venture into a banana grove belonging to the villagers would be shot with a poisoned arrow so lethal that a single scratch would lead to paralysis and imminent death.

After leaving Walikare, the only refugees able to eat were those who had a few coins. They would run a little mobile business, buy a little salt and then resell it in smaller quantities to the refugees who didn't want to eat their rice without salt. One would earn this rice by hard work, piling up bags of rice for the villagers. One cup of de-husked rice would be the payment for piling up 100kg.

Some refugees, those who still had a little sorghum (a kind of cereal) from the last camp, would try to grind it on rocks or on the asphalted road connecting Bukavu to Kisangani and passing through Walikare. Most of these refugees came from the area to the north, Byumba and Ruhengeri, and were accustomed to this kind of displacement ever since October 1990 when the RPF attacked Rwanda from Uganda. With flour obtained this way—inevitably mixed with dust and dirt—a broth would be prepared and sold to other refugees who still had the means to pay with a few coins.

Others launched a business selling *imishaba* (long, green bananas). *Imishaba* or plantain, were cooked with cassava in palm oil, which is abundant in the region. Each piece sold for 10,000 Zairian francs. Others sold a palm wine called *libondo*. They bought it from the Zairians who extracted it from the trunk of palm trees. It was a whitish sap which, when left to ferment for quite some time, produced a wine. One glass sold for 50 Zairian francs. Since the soldiers lived in the camps, they were also aware of which refugees sold items to other refugees. The refugees, who had nothing to sell and no money to buy food, ate the fruit of palm trees either raw or cooked. In addition to this, a refugee with no money could also eat green or ripe fruit, if lucky enough to find any along this road where nothing grew. Some people braved going into the fields of the Zairians to search for sweet or bitter cassava. Many of them paid for these with their blood. Refugees did what they had to in order to survive in these very difficult times. The Zairians, including the Zairian Military, would kill the refugees for this. Some refugees resorted to imitating the tactics of the *Yakaa awa* (Zairian Military) who terrorized, mistreated or massacred them. These soldiers could inflict the death penalty on a refugee if he still had something valuable in his possession, such as a plastic mat given to him by the HCR in a previous camp.

At times we would see a fight between the discontented refugees. The winner would get a chicken or pods of manioc which would then be inevitably confiscated by the soldiers from Zaire. These contingents of soldiers, who were once ordered by the UN to guard the refugee camps, actually fanned the fires of discontent and misery. I came across a former hotel owner in the refugee camp of Mugunga, a Mr. Moto Moto, who owned a hotel made of plastic tarps. The Military Contingents—members of zccs: Zairian Contingent for Camp Security—had forced him to undress and took his clothes in exchange for others. They thoroughly searched his clothing but he had expected this and had given his money to another refugee, one that they wouldn't suspect. This type of abuse is probably another reason, besides the one of fear of infiltration, that they prevented us from entering their camp and mixing with their inhabitants.

I took advantage of this stop to secretly enter the camp where food and other aid were given to the unaccompanied children or *Enfants Non Accompagnés* –ENA– those who had lost their parents or been abandoned by them. If a child had by chance survived, this camp would offer a place of refuge. They were few who survived parental abandonment. The food was good but, sadly, it didn't last long. Just as I was getting used to the milk, broth, and cookies from the NGO, the camp was once again destroyed.

This destruction took place several days after Madame Sadako Ogata, then Commissioner of the UNHRC, visited. This happened in spite of her promise of protection by the UNHRC. Either this Japanese woman did not keep her word, or she was an accomplice to the deceitful intentions of Mr. Gasana Anastase, then Rwandan Minister of Foreign Affairs and Co-operation. He did his utmost to convince the International Community that there were no Rwandan refugees left on Zairian soil. If he would have at least allowed the International Community to intervene and save thousands of Burundian refugees and persons protected according to the terms of the Geneva Convention of 1959, the plan to totally exterminate Rwandan refugees would have been derailed! I think that, today, he regrets the outcome of the statement of guarantee made by his ridiculous proclamation. The result was the massacre of people of his own ethnic group, the Hutu compatriots. He posed as a Tutsi, not any Tutsi but one from Canaan, which means from Uganda, as they call themselves to distinguish from the Tutsi from Zaire, Burundi, or from inside Rwanda. The Tutsi government put a lid on his lying and treason.

However, the protection that the Commissioner of the UNHCR had been promising came only with the definitive destruction of the refugee camps in Zaire, as well as massacres designed to eliminate all Hutu refugees from the land of the living. They had to pursue them wherever they were to be found and wherever cremation of the bodies would be possible. The High Commission for Refugees (HCR), of which Sadako Ogata was Secretary General, did nothing to warrant the attack by Rwanda against the refugee camps of Kivu South. They remained silent during these same attacks against the camps of the north and, even when the refugees were pursued in the jungle and forced to wander without issued goods, the UNHRC said there were no refugees left on Zairian soil.

It was only when Sadako arrived at Tingi-Tingi that she confessed to the error. Sadly, after she left, the camp was totally destroyed, and survivors of the massacre wandered again without the help of the UNHRC. Help would come in May, June, July, and August 1997 to repatriate the undying—the *immortal,* in the sense that all means to kill them had failed. These were repatriated, according to what UNHRC called *voluntary repatriation* but was in actuality 100% forced. Did Sadako still think that no refugees were to be found on Zairian soil? I think so!

THE OMINOUS SIGNS—The events of this day are forever engraved in my memory. To ever forget it seems impossible. Something extraordinary occurred. It was the first time I ever saw an airplane have an accident, and not just any accident, let me tell you. In the morning, a plane, attempting to land at the Tingi-Tingi airport, decapitated a woman who was carrying a baby on her back. Thank goodness the plane could no longer fly; it had died as well. Nevermind that it had just killed two refugees!

On the same day, another plane from Caritas, that was bringing the supplies to us, got a flat tire. An airplane with a flat tire! This was perhaps another sign, a foreshadowing of what would later be confirmed as an historic carnage. As well, on the same day, a military PUMA helicopter had a breakdown and wasn't able to maintain altitude. So, a plane from Kenya came to transport the rich and the Protestant pastors. Happy were the rich who were able to escape the calamity that would befall us!

I had already eavesdropped information from the officers who were exchanging intelligence on the state of the war. I learned that the camp was about to fall. The rebels had already circled it. I had to warn the refugees to flee and to head for Lubutu. Since I already knew which road to take, with great anticipation I headed out in that direction. The villagers were waiting for us on the bridge and barred the path. They began killing us. Since I am an expert in infiltration, I slipped into the brush and watched for an opportune time to traverse. In this way, I was able to escape the vigilant villagers who impeded entry into their city. My child was quiet. I had some milk with me that I had kept since we had been in the camp. With the child on my back and the help of a plastic jug, I swam to the other bank of the evil river. I was proud of myself for being among those rare refugees to cross without incident. I had been successful in achieving what most would not, and their life would end on the shore or in the river. Beyond the river, food provisions had been set aside for refugees. They were being guarded by the Zairian military who were preventing any refugees from arriving at this destination. The soldiers, after destroying and pillaging the provisions, took the road to Kisangani, staying as far away as possible from the combat zone. They handed us over to our compatriots who pounced on us like a wolf on lambs! It was about a 400 km trek on an asphalt road. Once again, my diminutive size allowed me to slip in among the villagers and to move along with them. Before leaving, I became an expert looter, taking boxes of cookies and bags of powdered milk. I stockpiled to later sell them to the fugitives who were streaming by in great numbers into the town of Lubutu. Sadly, I watched them cross the Lubutu River as I had done the night before. The customary community leaders, in collusion with the rebels, were holding them back. A few days beforehand, any refugee who had attempted to put one foot in the city had been killed. And so it was impossible for the refugees to know what had been plotted against them. They had to wait until the entire camp was emptied and all the refugees had gathered around the bridge.

In the meantime, the rebels who, a long time beforehand, had infiltrated the city, organized an attack specifically against the refugees gathered on the Lubutu bridge. Some were ahead of them while others attacked them from behind as they left camp. When the plans were executed, shots rang out from every direction. The target was clearly the crowd of refugees. Afraid, and en masse, the refugees made a mad dash to cross the river. Some swam, some walked over the bridge or on the heads of those who had already gone into the water. A bomb destroyed the bridge and killed those who were on or under it. It was an absolute stampede and each person managed as best he could. Woe to the little children, the sick, the weak, and especially the pregnant women! Misery fell also upon the men who had looted the supplies at Tingi-Tingi. There was great loss of human life. These looters were shaken down by assailants and hurled into the water thereby forced to begin crossing. Unfortunately, they overtook the others. As the shower of bombs continued in the area, the refugees panicked and threw themselves into the river. To swim? Not at all! They were so numerous that swimming was impossible. Those who had first gone into the water formed a bridge for the others. A great number of people perished in the Lubutu River and surrounding area. Even those who had managed to cross over had to abandon all their possessions.

One man's misfortune is another's good fortune. I made $200 on the items I had looted. Unfortunately, after only two days, I was stripped of the money. A wolf became lamb for another and the human became too inhumane. They didn't even take pity on me, child that I was. Why didn't they have compassion for the child that I carried on my back who needed their help? It was every man for himself. I wanted, in revolt, to go back. Sadly though, I was aware of what was going on behind us, namely more killings and murders! I didn't know what to do. In despair, I set out to follow these refugee wolves, and at the same time, I was careful to stay as far away as possible from those blood thirsty rebel compatriots who were killing us. During the executions, they even mocked us in our maternal Kinyarwanda to make us understand that we shared the same blood except that ours was to be spilled while theirs was preciously spared.

What an injustice! What cruelty! It really doesn't matter, for it's better to die tomorrow than today. It's still better to stay alive with an empty stomach than to die satiated. Moreover, I would tell myself: *"Ntankuba ikubita umunyabugingo"* (Lightning cannot strike a person to whom God has still extended life!)

Everyone thought only of himself. At the Lubutu River, I saw women cast off their babies so that they could cross more freely. It was grave! As for me, I was never tempted to abandon my little brother, even though he weighed heavily. We headed out toward

Kisangani during the night to avoid potential rebel infiltration. We didn't know that the rebels were already ahead of us. I can vouch for that because I had been able to cross over long before. The assailants had mingled with the refugees so that they could advance together and lead them to the slaughterhouse known only to them. We had regrouped into small teams so that we could move ahead more easily.

I remember that, along the road, the rebels who had infiltrated our group would pull some refugees to the side of the road and then we would hear their screams. They were undoubtedly stabbed to death. The formation in small groups actually facilitated their operation. Besides that danger, we had to cover 60 km per day because we were being followed by the rebels in their vehicles and we were on a good asphalted road. The presence of people among us wearing military uniforms brought much harm to us. These soldiers created confusion because some rebels also wore military attire while others wore civilian clothes like us. I was among those who brought up the rear. I had become a specialist in the art of hiding. Actually, since I had to walk barefoot on an asphalted road, I decided that it was better to walk at night while the refugees slept and the road didn't burn my poor feet, which had been so abused from travelling an unbelievable distance. During the daytime, I would hide in the brush, not far from the roadway so that I wouldn't get lost. Another advantage was the protection of my baby from the unbearable sun of Kisangani. It was so hot that women were even allowed to walk, stripped naked to the waist.

It was also interesting to watch the pretty girls with their long locks of hair, curiously full of lice, and whose beautiful breasts, always pointing straight ahead, were exposed to the sun. Their nails had been ripped off by the trees in the jungle and their feet were pitted with holes from the heat of the asphalted road upon which we trod. Some of the girls covered their feet with palm or banana leaves. With these they made a sort of slipper that we call *ingata*. Some were lucky enough to be carried on the backs of their fiancés, friends, or brothers. It was amusing to see a grown girl or woman on the back of a man.

I preferred walking at night in order to avoid all of this. I moved ahead, at times, with the assailants. I was too little to be noticed. In this way, I heard all that was said in Kinyarwanda, the language spoken by the rebels as well as Swahili and English. This is how I came to know of their macabre plans. I learned that they already had spies on the banks of the Ubundu River and others on the bridge several kilometres before entering the city of Kisangani so as to gather us together at this giant river. Thus, a single bomb would be enough to exterminate this entire mass of refugees. We tried to avoid death but death pursued us everywhere. Thanks to my nocturnal movements, I had access to a lot of information that other refugees, perhaps, did not. The changing of the military guard occurred evidently at night. One must not forget that the infiltrators walked among us as well. They passed for refugees even though they were the ones who, at a precise moment, would eliminate us. That's curious, isn't it? Their role was to slow down the refugees en route to Kisangani thus giving the rebels behind them time to get organized. The refugees were discouraged and had lost their zest for life. They had, for some time, been infiltrated by the rebels whose purpose was stirring-up disturbances, muddling and inciting fear among them. This led to total discouragement and a lack of confidence in the leaders, the former chiefs of the camps. On this last point they didn't achieve 100% success.

At Kilometre 82, something unexpected occurred, just as we were beginning to look forward to entering Kisangani. Hope was being expressed in the singing of melancholic songs alternating with songs of praise to Our God Sabaoth, Lord of Armies—we might have asked which ones!

We heard for example, *"Joziana weeeee, Joziana weeeee, tuzahurira kwa Data"* (Oh, Josiana, oh Josiana, we will meet in Heaven) –and– *"Wowe wambukije ab'Isiraheli, ukabageza Kanahaniiii, ngaho natwe tuyobore"* (You, who have guided all of Israel, You led them to Canaan, lead us as well).

We sang like those slaves who had to pass before Caesar in Ancient Rome before dying—"Ave Caesar..." Just as those slaves had been tormented by fear of death, we were also tortured by fear of a horrible death, since, at this point, death seemed inevitable. To sing was to be distracted from what was going on. The time to be shot would come without warning. Imagine tens of thousands of refugees hopelessly singing in unison. Why? I could say that each of us was nourished by the hope of escaping from these bullies and arriving in Kisangani. However, that hope lasted no longer than the morning fog. We were surprised to learn that the rebels were already ahead of us on the bridge at the entrance to the city of Kisangani. However, I was not surprised. I knew that there were rebels on the bridge over the Zaire River at Kisangani. I had warned the other refugees, but they didn't believe me. My warnings were put aside as childish. They died, for as we say in our language, "*Amatwi arimo urupfu ntiyumva*" (the air filled with death never listens). No one would be able to enter Kisangani without crossing the bridge except by boat!

This river is so immense that large boats are an absolute necessity. To escape, we headed toward the Ubundu, one of the streams nearest the Zaire River. It was at this point that those who were soldiers or Interahamwe were asked to separate themselves immediately from the rest of the refugees. The separation was made quickly with the exception of the soldiers who refused to abandon their families. They were, however, forced to surrender all weapons. This time I was with the refugees, since the assailants with whom I had walked at night, had passed everyone to wait for us on the bridge. There, something even more cruel was being prepared, something that forced me to join the ranks of the refugees. I hurried to leave among the first ones. How did I succeed in doing so? As they were regrouping us into small teams and we were walking in single file, I removed myself from the ranks. I had to, in effect, deviate but 50 m from the common road while always maintaining the same direction. Whenever I started to wander, I was able to find the right direction by listening to the voices and the cries of refugees heading toward Ubundu. By moving along apart from the others, I had certain advantages, but certain risks were also heightened. We were always in the jungle, even if there were a few homes scattered here and there.

It wasn't easy to find food. I could only pick wild berries. I ate them without any concern for what was edible or not. I didn't know how to differentiate them. I assumed that everything was edible and if I couldn't find any fruit, I didn't worry one bit. I was used to eating snails that I found on the ground.

As we approached the Ubundu River, rotting fruit was found in abundance. In any case, we didn't run out of garbage to fool our stomachs. We had no worries about tomorrow. Every day was filled with enough hardship and our hope for life was renewable in a second! A few kilometres from the Ubundu River, I began coming upon corpses of refugees. They had been thrown far from the road. I knew for sure that they had been refugees because their arms and legs had been bound to their back just like the numerous bodies I had come across from the time I left the camp at Katale until my arrival at Tingi-Tingi. I got scared. I decided to rejoin the other refugees. I didn't realize that I had already passed them. They had stopped a kilometre away from the river. I had already reached the river.

I was being treated like *mwana mboka* (a Congolese subject). I was able to advance to the far extremity of the ad hoc camp. I was so dirty that I looked a lot like the villagers around that river where laundry was done and baths taken, always without soap. Once, during the night, I slipped into the camp to find out what was happening. Inside, refugees were dying from hunger, fatigue and injuries. There was no one to care for them. With what supplies? These poor refugees had no quality of life. I decided to backtrack. At least there, I would be able to spend the night in little fishing huts on the bank of the Ubundu. From there, I could see some of the rebels who came to negotiate deals with the native Zairians. This is how one party of rebels made it across. Another party had infiltrated the groups of refugees. I recall that, over a period of several weeks, some refugees negotiated deals with local authorities but were never actually given permission to cross the Ubundu River. The refugees were molding there, eyes peeled on the river that they had no right to approach. Exception had been made for a few leaders of the refugees, the negotiators. I would've loved to have revealed this to the refugees, the fact that they were actually negotiating with the rebels. They wouldn't have believed me. I knew who they really were. They almost always came to the river to make plans to block the crossing of refugees.

Since I was able to get by well enough in Swahili, I had the opportunity to enter into a conversation with a villager, and I managed to convince him that I was Zairian. I told him that I was a Mukuru from Tingi-Tingi. I was sure that I wouldn't be found out. I told him that these refugees had decimated all my family. This villager took us into his home located very near the river. He taught me to swim, to fish and to row. He felt sorry for me. Unfortunately, good things don't last very long! I don't know how, but one of the assailants, disguised as a villager, managed to fool me. He spoke to me in Kinyarwanda and I mistakenly answered him in Kinyarwanda, our mother tongue. He had found me out and wanted to kill me. He would have succeeded if my Zairian friend had not intervened. In his presence, I refused to speak again in Kinyarwanda. I spoke only Swahili and to further convince him, I attempted speaking in Lingala. The Zairian was convinced that I was not Rwandan. As far as he was concerned, I belonged to one of the Zairian tribes.

The Afandi, an officer who came to meet us, confirmed that I was in fact Rwandan. For that reason, I didn't have to return to the place where the refugees were gathered because I could have informed them of the impending plot. He began terrorizing me by kicking me. Had it not been for the intervention of the customary chief of this community, I would've been killed that day! He took me to his home because he believed that we shared the same Zairian blood. There were a lot of Rwandan infiltrators at his place. In order to stay in his home with them, I never spoke Kinyarwanda. I learned my lesson from the last experience. That's how I learned that they had rushed in some troops to Kilometre 52 and Kilometre 82 from Kisangani. Their mission was to massacre the refugees in due time. They were also planning an attack on the refugees who were assembled near the river. I got scared. I started to hoard my rations, being careful to put aside the *chikwanga* (a kind of dough that travels well), a secret, I'd learned in Lubutu.

D-Day would come. Everything was ready for the attack on the refugees. Provisions were to be dropped by parachute from a plane. Refugees would be assembled for the distribution of biscuits, corn flour, rice and peas. Then they would fire on them, forcing them to run toward the river. They were saying all this, ignorant of the plans being prepared, as well, by the refugees who were tired of stagnant negotiations. The refugees had just decided that they would cross the river, against the wishes of the villagers who wanted to keep them prisoners there. Some among the refugees were determined to cross, whatever the cost, and had just built rafts and makeshift boats from their plastic tarps. Some refugees gathered for the distribution while, at the same time, others went to the river to try crossing over. They came upon rebels who were organizing the attack. It was already a bad start and the plan fell apart. They were forced to attack, win or lose. Irate, the refugees were forced to begin crossing. Some used their rafts, others their plastic tarps with which they made a kind of a canoe. Some attempted to swim across. Where could they land? Not far away as the river was too wide. It was total stampede and absolute chaos. Mortars were spewing bombs on the refugees. The assailants, who were on the east side of the terrain where provisions were being distributed, were ready to pounce on the refugees who came their way, but didn't find very many clients. Nearly everyone had gathered at the river. How were they to get across? Some refugees searched for boats, some tried to negotiate one with the Zairian owners who had hidden them. And so, some who still had a little money, paid the villagers to take them across. Dollars were not acceptable currency. Actually, the villagers were not familiar with these green bills marked "in god we trust". Even if one were willing to pay $100 or $200, they wouldn't take you into their boats. Only clothing, soaps or a radio receiver were acceptable currency to buy passage by canoe.

I was personally shocked by the lack of solidarity among the refugees. Everyone wanted to cross first. Perhaps solidarity is lost once the vision of the common good—the country—is lost. I don't know. I am extremely sorry that the weak and the sick were abandoned. At a certain moment, the strongest such as those who were rich or those soldiers who did not abandon their families and had hidden some weapons on themselves, appropriated these much sought-after boats. And so, to cross, one had to be related to an important officer. I remember a woman and her husband who appointed himself captain in order to seize a sergeant's boat. What was going on? The so-called sergeant had boarded all of his family. At the moment that the boat was leaving shore, another young man appointed himself captain to force the first one to turn around. "Sergeant," he told him, "your family is to disembark. My family will go to the other shore of the river first. Understand?"

"Yes sir," He replied, and to demonstrate his compliance, he immediately had his own family get out of the boat in order to take on the family of the so-called captain. The law of the jungle ruled. Refugees who had nothing to barter, tried to swim across. I swear to you that not one of them escaped drowning or the waterfalls that are particularly dangerous at this location.

In the meantime, the assailants continued their dirty work of executing defenceless refugees. The pillaging with heavy arms continued. Other refugees, in desperation, tried to cross on the plastic tarps they had fashioned into a canoe. Two pieces of wood in the shape of a cross were used to support the tarps and form a sort of a canoe. Anyway, only one out of ten who attempted the impossible made it to the other shore. The Ubundu River, tributary of the Zaire River—the 2nd largest river on the planet after the Amazon—has a very rapid current. Even the wooden boats of the adventurous paddlers were swallowed up in the falls, to be forever lost. I won't forget the dozens of Burundian refugees who gathered around their burgomaster Mustanteri and together climbed onto a raft only to disappear in the famous falls that gobbled up so many refugees. "The Ubundu is not like Lake Tanganyika that has no rapid current or waterfalls", said those who watched them disappear forever. As for our team, God was on our side! We survived this perilous situation. Death refused us that day.

I knew how to swim very well but I couldn't swim across the river with my little brother on my back. I didn't have the endurance. I thought that if I threw myself into the water some goodhearted people would possibly come to my aid and would take us into their boat. I hesitated to do it. I didn't trust anyone. I ran along the shore looking for someone who would take me into his boat or onto his raft or sheetings. I had travelled a great distance, running back and forth, and I was already tired and beginning to lose hope. A villager, who had seen me in the Zairian village, took me into his boat, believing that I simply wanted to get to the opposite shore.

On the other side of the river of death, life was found in abundance. There was food there. But anyone who tarried, risked his life. We would rest only after three hours of walking. It was nighttime and we had already arrived in another centre far from the route that leads to Kisangani. It is there that we spent the night. We awakened very early in the morning, and after having prepared some *sosoma* (a broth made of soya, sorghum, and corn), we regained our path which led us mainly through the jungle. We walked day and night trying to escape our compatriot predators. I loved walking in the dark of night where we would come upon animals that proved to be less ferocious than the men in our pursuit.

This helped me a great deal. Even today, I'm not afraid of the night. At night, I guide the bandits. And the proprietors of Kigali love to send me to get their *indaya* (prostitutes). They pay me a lot of money—500 FR—when I bring them a young one of my age. Also, when we guarded the buffalo, or *Twaragiye imbogo,* which means we've not had anything to eat all day, I had to steal during the night or sometimes serve as guide for the bandits in order to bring back food. This is how my companion Mayibobo get food to eat. They love me a lot, these little commandos.

Once, we left the city around 7 pm to go to *Giti cy' inyoni* about 8 km west of the city centre. We were going to get bananas and sugar cane. I was the chief of the gang. You see, we were on the verge of death, dying of hunger. I am not afraid of the dark or of the animals. Whenever I meet dogs, they run away. I like that. I am terrible, I am. They call me chief of the gang. All of this is due to the endurance I exhibited during the adventure in the jungles of the Congo when I was trying to escape this horde of men, men thirsty for innocent blood. I'm not afraid of anything. To go walking in the night is both habitual and familiar. What do you expect? When the police took us to Gikongoro, thereby preventing us from living in the capital, within three days I was back. We walked, without rest, day and night. It was a child's game for us, and we were accustomed to it. We know how to endure hunger and fatigue. We don't need a house or bed to sleep in. We are even capable of sleeping on a rock. We can spend the night in torrential rains without any problem, with the help of some hemp and special glue, a drug available to us. What do you expect? We were accustomed to this situation, our situation. Rwandan society, in killing our parents, had made us Mayibobo and excluded us as well.

In as much as this society has not asked our forgiveness and has not re-established the dignity denied to us by its wickedness, all it considers doing for us in the future is in vain. For that matter, why don't they want to partner with us to seek the solution to our problem? I find it funny! Look at history, and you will see that there was a time when the Mayibobo posed no problem. Didn't the problem only start with the October war at Byumba? Was it not provoked by those who hounded us and massacred us in the darkest depths of the equatorial jungle of Zaire, the first who killed our parents since October 1990? Were the first spoiled fruit of society not the children of Byumba who were displaced from Kagitumba to Nyacyonga when the RPF Inkotanyi attacked the Country of a Thousand Hills? Were they not the first to appear in the city of Kigali searching for food? What would you answer them, you the people of Kigali? Go see Kinani—Kinani was the nickname of President Habyarimana, accused by you of being the instigator of the October war. I was but a child, one year old! Just know that we, street kids, have a strong solidarity in that we inform each other of everything. We are lucky to have among us the first Mayibobo of Kigali, the pioneers from Byumba and those kids who served as RAP's soldiers known under nickname of "Kadogo". They help us a lot. We are planning a 15th Anniversary of our existence in 2005, and we invite you now, but please do not come bearing arms or with judgement in your mind.

ON THE ROAD TO KISANGANI

It was at Obilo that the rebel plans came to fruition. Obilo is situated 52 km from Kisangani. Obilo became the stage for the most vicious murders and massacres of all time. The refugees, tired of being in the huge jungle where there was nothing to eat, arrived here more than worn out, but somewhat hopeful, because there is a railway station here.

They hoped that some type of intervention would eventually take place by the International Community who had, so far, forgotten them. Forgotten even by the French government, in whom we had placed our trust, ever since they had saved us from the protests of the enraged soldiers of the RPF at Inkotanyi, in 1994 when the "Turquoise Zone" was created. It reminded me of the time that we had picked up the pace to arrive at Walikare because the Zairians had told us that the French and the UNHCR officers were waiting for us with food, clothes and medications, as was being offered in the other refugee camps. But then, instead of coming to our aid, the planes—perhaps the UNHCR—swooped down upon us. Planes over our heads were a sign that bombs would soon be surging down upon us. It was not long before Walikare deceived us as well. At the 12 km marker, precisely at the aerodrome, they crammed us together like ants to wait for so-called eventual help. In lieu of this, we became targets for intensified bombings. This put an end to our hope, hope renewed since Rukwi, the last camp for surviving refugees from Katale and Kahindo. The amazing thing is that during that time Radio Rwanda loudly claimed on the air that no Rwandan refugees remained on Zairian soil. An out and out lie! And the UNHCR who were supposed to be coming to our aid turned a deaf ear. Maybe they didn't want to contradict the Kigali government (their best friend), who had deafened the International Community with word that all refugees from Zaire had re-entered Rwanda. It was probably a plan to massacre all of us without anyone knowing. In affirming our non-existence, the revanchist plan of the government of Kigali reached its greatest wish: to eliminate all Hutu refugees found on Zairian soil.

At Tingi-Tingi, Emma Bonino came to see us, but I'm not sure what her purpose was. She only made some of us cry (of course those who still had tears). She told us that she had just made the sad discovery of refugees living in deplorable conditions. The government of Kigali had denied, up until that time, the existence of any refugees, and evidently the International Community backed them up! Kigali stood by its spokesperson of the time, Mr. Gasana Anastase, Minister of Foreign Affairs—himself presently a refugee in the USA—and also by the star performer of the government, Mr. Bizimungu Pasteur, then President of the Republic in name only. These two bought-off Hutus echoed the statement of the government by affirming, without any shame or remorse, that no Rwandan refugees were to be found on Zairian soil. Mr. Bizimungu Pasteur reaffirmed this even though he knew that his own father was among the refugees who had not yet re-entered the country! At least Bonino's tears got us some food and medical aid.

What can I say about Mrs. Sadako Ogata, the High Commissioner of the United Nations for Refugees, who came to Tingi-Tingi only a few days after Mrs. Emma Bonino's visit? Her departure from Tingi-Tingi was not followed by assistance in the way of food, medication, or protection, but by the final destruction of the surviving refugee camps at Amisi and Tingi-Tingi. The pursuit of refugees, even beyond the borders of Zaire, one could say, was the result of this trip of the Japanese Mrs. Sadako. What did the UNHCR do upon finally learning of our existence in the Zairian jungle? Only God knows the reason for this abandonment, and He knows what He will one day ask of this illustrious defender of human rights, Mrs. Sadako Ogata (at the time of our martyr she had already been awarded with a medal as a champion of human rights as we can see on http://www.un.org.news/dh/hlpanel/ogata-bio.htm. Nevertheless, she was not ignorant of the role of the HCR in regard to refugees: "The statute of the HCR clearly establishes the work of the organization to be humanitarian and apolitical. This work is based on two principle, tightly bound functions: the protection of refugees and a search for lasting solutions to their problems."

Let's go back to the carnage at Bialo, this place that refused to uphold the hope of surviving refugees who had once been saved from the murders and massacres perpetrated in Masisi, Walikare, Tingi-Tingi, Lubutu, Kilometre 82 in Kisangani, Ubundu, around the Lualaba River, and the slaughterhouse aboard the *gari ya moshi* (the train that transported the refugees to Kisangani). The refugees hoped, in vain, for a quick intervention by the International Community. Would this intervention ever come about? Our bullies had seen to everything. They were supported, it seemed, by everyone! Sure that no help would be forthcoming, and assured also of the passive complicity of the Zairian army because of their incapacity to intervene, those who were annihilating us took their time in killing the refugees. We had been forsaken by the whole world. We found ourselves in a place named Kilometre 52. The rebels had just taken hold of Kisangani. They were, therefore, able to attack us all the way from Kisangani to our future destination. And so, we were tortured from all sides. Behind us, the assailants pursued us, and before us, they awaited in ambush. Lord, what have we done to deserve such a sentence! Some refugees, having heard about the fall of Kisangani, decided to take another road, thrusting them deeper into the jungle, in the hope that they might escape certain and imminent death. We found ourselves either at Opala or at Ikela, two cities that today are building on the graves of thousands of refugee bodies.

We were sure of at least one thing: finding water in the dense jungle. And, in fact, there was water—more than we needed—since it is there that a lot of rivers like the Lomami, feed into the Zaire River. They are tributaries flowing into the Zaire before it reaches the Atlantic Ocean that we were slowly approaching. The Lomami and the Zaire claimed many of our people. Indeed, besides those who starved to death, those chewed up by wild animals, or those who perished from injuries or illness, large numbers threw themselves into the waters of these rivers simply to avoid the brutal death they knew they would have to suffer, once captured. In this jungle, there was nothing to eat except fish that we could catch with our hands. We had to cross all these rivers, large and small, either by swimming across or by building rafts. It was very risky. That there were any survivors like myself and my child is truly a miracle. We had to eat fruit, edible or wild. We could not differentiate them. We chose them randomly, by feel, as we had before. Myself, I developed an art for choosing my fruit. Anything that wasn't bitter was edible.

Also, I changed my strategy for following the refugees, since we were in the middle of the jungle without any light. That, in and of itself, was a ray of sunshine. It was no longer a question of walking during the day or night. It was always as dark as night time in this shady jungle. We all slept at the same time and got up at the same time to continue journeying together. This way we felt protected— "An antelope that strays from the flock becomes gravy." We blindly tried to follow one another, sometimes not sure where to step because it was so dark in the jungle. However, this protection was not without inconveniences. Some people died of hunger because, if by chance we came upon a fruit tree, everyone rushed headlong to gather these fruits. Obviously the strongest ones did not show consideration for the weak.

I loved the system we had devised to cross rivers. On occasion, there would be two or three small boats. In single file, we were placed in these delightful boats belonging to the villagers. There were no exceptions to this golden rule; first aboard were the soldiers and their families who, on a positive note, were to offer protection in the event of an attack by the villagers on either side who might act savagely because of our mass presence. But I can understand where they were coming from. We were not on a march for peace. We ravaged everything we found along the way: chickens, goats, pigs, fruit, corn, etc.

These villagers were good warriors and hunters. They lived off the land, hunting, fishing and cultivating corn and manioc. Don't ask them what a dollar looks like. They would be insulted. They were not preoccupied with covering their nakedness. They had no knowledge of clothing and didn't need any to protect themselves from the cold. They were accustomed to this austere primitive lifestyle. It's understandable that they didn't welcome us with open arms. They attacked us, perhaps thinking that they had found new prey. We had to fight them off a few times so that we could continue our march, always aware of the swords, guns, grenades and bombs behind us. Their operators were thirsty for our blood. Survival instinct infers that the weak attack the weaker and so, we often had to fight against these villagers when they tried to prevent us from passing through their villages. They had good reason to battle against us. If we should, by happenstance, find ourselves in their manioc field, now there was a feast for the refugees! There was partying in the village. We had fish, so then, what were we lacking? It was a meal fit for a king, manioc bread and fish, though cooked without oil and salt. No problem for us. Only one thing mattered: anything to trick the stomach. Anyway, this meal tasted better than the leaves and fruit of the jungle that had become our daily diet. Oh my Lord! It was such a grand feast! At times, in order to stave off disease and to regain our strength, we had eaten *isombe* (manioc leaves). We tried to dilute them so that they would last longer. Thanks to them, we could speed up, at last, to arrive at huge fields of corn. Hurray! We were saved from starvation. We ate corn boiled, grilled and in *impungure* (seeds that were dried, then cooked).

Solidarity among the refugees was beginning to crumble. We no longer advanced in organized groups because some stayed behind to gather more corn, manioc and fish. Sadly, they paid the price with their blood. Many of them were summarily massacred by the assailants. At this time, myself and my little brother felt spoiled. We ate raw corn, and we also ate of the stalks, sucking on them to get the sugar out. It was succulent. One might say, real sugarcane! I tried to bundle up a faggot for my supply. I would take one stem that I ground between my teeth and then give it to my little brother who had no teeth. As far as the corn, I would take the kernels, grind them on the stones and then take the juice and give it to my little brother. He didn't know how to chew anything. I would chew it for him and he would swallow whatever I had chewed or ground up. It was quite amusing, you see!

MASSACRE IN THE VICINITY OF KISANGANI

Who could ignore the massacres committed along the road to Kisangani, even if the bodies had been burned? The truth was not what one would have the people believe. The truth is carved out in the act of massacring. Even if the murderers wanted to kill and bury the truth, it lives on eternally and is etched in the memory of those who witnessed these atrocities with their own eyes. We must believe it. Even if the corpses were burned, the innocence of those killed 7 km from Kisangani cries out for vengeance before God. The chase of survivors, dispersed in the forest following the destruction of the camps at Kasese and Obilo, intensified by the help of dogs, will never be erased from the memory of those few survivors. The local population, disguised under the insignia of the Red Cross, terrorized by the cruelty of our compatriots and used like wolves to hunt down refugees, will one day witness to the truth. Unless, they too, were not wiped out in the aftermath. Under the insignia and flag of the Red Cross, the locals furrowed through the forest in search of refugees. Anyone who trusted in the integrity of the Red Cross insignia and came out of hiding, was soon lynched. The asphalted road to Kisangani was blockaded by our compatriots, Rwandans of RAP and choked with the bodies of their own people, or should I say, their ashes, since their bodies were burned. Forced to be accomplices to the military, this population dirtied their hands. I don't carry a grudge against them because they, as well, wanted to escape the wickedness of our assassins.

The die had been cast. Evidently, they wanted to be finished with the refugee affair. Everything had been readied for this dirty work. "You want to murder us in the forest?" asked the refugees at the moment of their execution. "Kill us here," they insisted, "and the white men of the HCR will be able to find our bodies."

The poor victims still believed in an intervention by the HCR and the International Community. They were crushed like ants, without any help, according to the perfectly planned, murderous plot of their foes. Anyone who had not been able to flee on time had lost a rare chance. The combing of the area was followed by shots fired from machine guns. The skulls of every person lying helplessly on the ground were shattered by the butt of a gun or a worn down hoe. The lightning-swift ordeal lasted only a few minutes. At nearly the same moment in time, an airplane circled the area, and I believe the pilot could have realized what was going on even if he were being fired at. The bulldozer dug a pauper's grave to swallow up the ashes of all the murdered bodies, burned out of necessity. The bullies, however, were not aware of the existence of several "Moses" who were hiding under some fresh bodies. When the HCR agents wanted to go to this site, they were denied access by soldiers who declared the area had become a "Red Zone" and therefore inaccessible. It was the first time the Rwandan soldiers had told the truth. Yes, this zone had become red—*red with the blood of Rwandans and Burundians!*

The survivors of this massacre can be counted on one's fingertips. Among them is one of my Mayibobo friends. He is the one who told us all of this. He has a scar on his lip from a bullet he took at the time. He's a real commando, that one. We love him a lot. He's the next in command after me. His speciality is organizing Sit-ins like the one we participated in at the Red Light in Nyabugogo until we got what we were asking for from the police, who were harassing us. We showed them what we are capable of. We are so closely united that one man's problem is the whole group's problem. The Mayibobo family is composed of all ethnic groups, even the Batwa who are excluded from the other two gangs. You see! Our solidarity is based on a common cause: fighting for our survival because society wants us dead. We are rejected by them because we act as a mirror. Through our misery can be seen the misery of all our society. Are we not the immediate result of its tearing apart? And yet, we live in perfect harmony. What do they need to follow our example? Evidently, unity is impossible for a nation rotten with egoism and the desire to dominate. There is the strongest need for them to be purified of their egoism. Ego is at the root of all these misunderstandings and armed conflicts, and yet, what do I know? If only this bloodshed had not produced orphans, widows, poor, and outcasts of society. Whoever wants to save Rwanda must, therefore, bandage up the social fibre and have a high-reaching degree of patriotism, a real patriotism, not just lip service. To those who speak of peace with their tongue only—look at all the false information spread by them through the international media even until now—while in reality brought the war into action by killing others and burning their bodies, it is time to tell them: "That's enough! Rwanda has suffered enough from hatred and exclusivity dating back to the time of monarchical regimes until now. It's time to bandage the wounds. Let's not forget that hatred disrupts life, egoism destroys a whole nation, only love and tolerance can rebuild this degenerated society."

What would be the future of a nation that produces greedy men, day in and day out? It buys its grave at a cheap price. And what would destroy this country even more is not these wars—as much in the exterior as in the interior of this jewel of a country—but the indifference of those who today feel provided for in material comforts. They are forgetting that all of that lasts no longer than the morning haze when it is not shared and that many before them possessed these good things too. The case of Félicien Kabuga should be an example to them. Once enjoying the richest status in Rwanda, he has become the most hunted man in the country and cannot freely and peacefully enjoy his possessions.

MASSACRES IN THE EQUATORIAL JUNGLE

The crossing of this large forest was not at all easy. The forest was very shady and every kilometre brought another stream to be crossed, by swimming or by boat. It was frightful. I later learned that this was the Equatorial Forest. I was happy to know that I had succeeded in a test worthy of a commando. I learned that, to be a soldier, not being afraid sufficed. If only I didn't hate warfare because of the cruelty we endured at the hands of the soldiers who pursued us, I could have become a good *Codo* (commando).

What qualifications am I lacking to become one? I have a high level of endurance. I have travelled all through Zaire on foot. Do you think that I am good at the military arts? The *Mucaka mucaka* (the morning run that the soldiers do for endurance training) does not scare me. For that matter, I sometimes have fun running with them. I keep up with them all the way, and often, I arrive before them. I'm still afraid of them for I know what they are capable of doing: killing.

I also have a lot of experience in crossing the enemy camp, even during the night. I admit that I am able to pursue the infiltrated Abacengezi, even to the depths of Zaire. I am not afraid of anyone or of death. I believe, moreover, that death scorns me because, time and time again, I could have been its prey. I can, therefore, challenge them because I'm an expert navigator in dense forest. I would, however, never want to be a guide for these soldiers. They would be so jealous of my expertise that they would kill me with one swift blow.

I do not like war. I remember what happened when the time came to cross the Lomami River. Since the Zairian soldiers demanded money to board the boat and I had none, I put my little brother into a bag. Then I asked one of the Zairian soldiers to take me on board with his family, on payment of my little pig in the bag—my little brother. Obviously, I kept the bag with me and prevented him from touching it because, in so doing, he would have discovered that it was a small child. My little guy never cried anymore. He knew very well that there was no one to cry to, since babies cry to elicit affection and comfort from their mothers.

Who would care about a Mayibobo like me? That's why I never cry anymore. My little brother knows very well that he mustn't cry. On the contrary, we must be always smiling. That is our life. And so, since I never manifested any fear and was always smiling, the Zairian officer didn't clue into the trick that I was playing on him. Maybe he was waiting to confront me on the other shore, to ensure that he would receive his little pig. Once we arrived on the other side of the giant waterway, at least an hour later, the Major did claim payment of his little pig. I gently took my bag, slowly untied it, hoping he would get impatient and let me go. As I watched his eye staring at me, I took out my little brother. Surprised, the officer asked me if that was the little pig. Indignant, he intimidated me by saying in Lingala, *"Yo peti na ngai, koseka na ngai te. Nakoboma yo"* (Hey little one, don't play with me. I can kill you). I understood Lingala but didn't want to answer him. I had just spent several weeks walking with the soldiers. I was familiar with Lingala ever since our time spent in Amisi and Tingi-Tingi. Just as I sensed that he wanted to beat me black and blue, my little brother smiled innocently at him, a smile that would disarm anyone who had ever been a parent. At least his wife was moved with pity for my child. She was the first woman to show an interest in my little brother since mom's death. She took him into her arms, and realizing that the only clothes he wore, a loincloth and a little knitted sweater in tatters, were full of lice that he picked up in Tingi-Tingi, she took off his clothes and threw them into the river.

He was washed with soap, smothered in beauty cream and dressed in a little white cloth, a little pair of pants and a red and white jacket. How handsome he looked in his princely attire! All children are beautiful, I suppose, but poverty separates them. This good Samaritan had dressed him like a prince. She gave me nothing. That's the breaks! She had no clothing in my size. Her only children were both two years old because they were twins.

The Major kept quiet, not saying a word. But finally, he said one thing to me in Lingala:

"*Oyebi lingala?*" (Do you understand Lingala?)

"*Moke moke,*" (a little) I responded, affirming the truth.

"*Oza refugié?*" (Are you a refugee?)

"*Naza refugié te, ngai naza mwana mboka,*" (I am not a refugee, I am a Zairian citizen) I told him, smiling to appear likeable.

"*Baboti ya mwana oyo baza wapi?*" (Where are this child's parents?) He asked me.

"*Bakufalaki na Lubutu,*" (They were killed near Lubutu) I replied, suddenly feeling nervous.

"*Mozalaki batu ya Maniema? Ozalaki ya ekolo gani?*" (Are you originally from Maniema, and of what tribe?)

"*Nazali motu ya Maniema no ekolo ya Bakumu.*" (I am from Maniema of the Bakumu tribe)

"*Nani obomaki baboti na bino?*" (Who killed your parents?)

"*Ba rebelles nde babomaki bango.*" (My parents were killed by the rebels)

"*Mwana tokosolaka kaka vengeance; Revanche na biso ekozolaka makasi koleka. Tokonyataka kaka mpe kotombola likoro mpene mpene na Kigali. Motu akobi kaka na katikati na bango nyonso te*" (Little one, we will seek revenge. Our revenge will be fierce. We will march on Kigali and no one will escape our beating!)

I thought, *You, you are no longer worth anything, good only for looting and running your legs off when the enemy arrives.* The refugees had given the Zairian soldiers the nickname *Mukamurenzi*, after a famous Rwandan woman athlete, a world-renowned cross country racer. To name them after her was a way to say that, instead of fighting and defending their country, they fled as fast as their legs would take them. On many occasions, I had seen them undressing, taking off their military uniform to avoid combat, and donning civilian clothes. If you had seen how many armoured cars they abandoned all along the road to Kisangani! They even left the mortars that the rebels later used to fire at us. These athletic soldiers were good for nothing.

I saw our officer approach the other soldiers to give them the order to spend the night there. He also gave the order to not allow any refugee to get past them. "The refugees are to follow us and not the other way around."

It was only later that I understood the reason for that interdiction. It was thanks to a conversation I overheard in Swahili that I came to know the whole affair: The bottom line was that there were two reasons that they didn't want the refugees to pass them: firstly, if the refugees passed by first, they would plunder the chickens, goats, and rice in the villages along the way. By the time the soldiers arrived, they would find nothing. Whenever soldiers passed, they always gathered up everything they could find: food, small and large animals and, of course, women. Secondly, the refugees served as a human shield, unwittingly protecting fleeing Zairian soldiers.

The refugees were aware that the rebels were just searching for them and not for the soldiers. Fearing death if they slowed their pace, these so-called refugees disregarded military orders. The refugees were accustomed to advancing at night, even if they didn't know where to go. One principle guided the refugees: to walk as far as possible and, if possible, to arrive at Kinshasa, at Mobutu's office. He was our last hope because he considered President Juvenal Habyarimana to be like a little brother, and Rwanda as a good friend of his country.

During the night, without the knowledge of the Zairian soldiers who had set up blockades to impede their progress and prevent them from getting ahead, the refugees began their walk toward infinity. They escaped to continue their adventure. They needed protection which wouldn't have been provided by the Zairian soldiers anyway. Also, walking ahead of them instead of behind was beneficial because they ravaged everything the refugees had. According to these soldiers, everything was a grenade, even a pair of pants or underwear still being worn. They stripped us of everything they called a grenade. This word was well understood to mean anything useful in the possession of a refugee. Since I had nothing on me, I wasn't in any danger. Would I benefit from some extraordinary favour? Filled with pity, the Major's wife asked her husband to allow us to travel with them.

She was very goodhearted to the point that she treated us like her own children. When she discovered that we were Rwandan, she was careful not to tell her husband. He was too mean toward Rwandans. He would not have allowed us to live, had he known we were Rwandans. We were lucky. The first night with them went marvellously well. However, I didn't sleep very well because I had taken a shower with soap and I had slept in a blanket. I didn't like blankets because I had not used one since my mother's death. I had been unable to carry it on my back along with my brother. I had grown used to spending the night without one, not even to protect myself from the cold.

When the Major awoke in the morning, having slept well in a nice house—without electricity of course, but in a bed—he found that all the refugees had left. Panic-stricken, he got into his head that he must have been captured by the rebels because those who should have protected him were gone. After eating manioc dough called *foufou* in military language, along with a chicken, he shared some with us as well. We were henceforth part of his family. The Major hurried us to leave this place.

According to the Major, the rebels were in the vicinity. To motivate his soldiers, "Tango" (one of many soldiers following him), made up information that the rebels were but a few steps away from us. They were in reality 1 km from the river, while we were on the opposite shore. As a tactic, some of the soldiers would have to stop the refugees from getting ahead. "The refugees must follow us and not the other way around," he told them.

Unfortunately, the refugees were already far ahead. Some had even headed toward Opala, the opposite direction from Ikela. These faced a sad misfortune because, once they arrived, rebels greeted them with the gallows. They massacred them mercilessly, without respite. Some of them were thrown into the Lomami River; others simply threw themselves in. They acted out of fear of the atrocities and tortures awaiting them, for they had witnessed the rebels inflicting pain on other refugees. Luckily, some were able to escape the vigilance of the flesh-hungry humans and sounded the retreat. But no matter how far they went, they would again meet rebel soldiers because they were all over.

At Opala, refugee blood soaked the soil, and vultures feasted on fresh human flesh. A good number of the refugees died in this place. Those who had taken the road back found that we were already gone. They had the bad luck of being greeted by the rebels who were pursuing us. The last straw was that the local population, who had become insensitive to the wickedness of the rebels, blocked the road so that we could not pass. It was to be expected. The few survivors who were successful in weaving their way through the forest, hurried to catch up to us. They were very lucky because the Zairian soldiers has already gone ahead of the refugees, thereby breaking their rhythm and making it so that those who had stayed behind would catch up to them. They were much protected and had managed to impose their own rhythm on the refugees. This was serious because the refugees were interested in organizing themselves and regulating the rhythm of their walk to escape the axe of the bullies. This strategy led to many deaths. Some were killed with mortars by rebels travelling by truck; others met a death by starvation because the Zairian soldiers ravaged everything in passing. When the soldiers were able to overtake the refugee lead, they appropriated everything that would have been food for the refugees.

Our Major and his soldiers were almost always drunk. They drank *libondo* (the local wine) or *kindingi* (dry alcohol) or *rutuku kanyanga* (ethanol) that the local population extracted from corn or manioc flour. Two sips were enough to get me drunk. Once, after having consumed a little bit of kindingi and some *bangi* (hemp), I fell down from a tree. I was trying to climb the tree in search of firewood. On my way down, I landed in the commando position. According to the Major, I would make a great commando. I felt absolutely no pain. I kept that word of the Major in my mind.

Since that day, I have taken to smoking hemp and drinking kanyanga. For me, a night without bangi is a night wasted; it gives me *amafri swingi nyinshi* (a tranquil, relaxed feeling). When I combine bangi (hemp) and kindingi (local vodka) I feel stronger than anyone in the world. I can take on anyone and accomplish anything.

To encourage me to make a career in the military, the Major gave me the job of carrying his Kalashnikov from time to time. It was obvious that I wasn't able to carry both the child and the gun. When the Major noticed this, he had me carry a grenade, and showed me how to handle it. That's when I started to change my focus. I forced myself to speak in Lingala to look like a true commando. I wouldn't back down before anyone. I thought of myself as a real Rambo.

The Major's wife was not pleased with my behaviour. I had become rude, unruly and arrogant. I had a *kingoma* (grenade) that gave me courage, and I was smoking up with the other soldiers. To change my behaviour, she revealed a secret to me. She told me that she, as well, was Rwandan. She had married this officer in Goma in 1994 as she was leaving Rwanda. In fact, they had lived together at Goma-ville, then at Munigi near the airport, and then at the military camp at Rumangabo. Not that long ago, they had been transferred to Kisangani. She also confided that her husband, as well, had Rwandan blood because his mother had come from Ruhengeri and that was why he had chosen to marry a Rwandan. She then advised me that, if I conducted myself politely and gently, she would guarantee my safe passage as far as *Kin* (Kinshasa, the capital of Zaire). She added that we would become their adopted children, and I would no longer have to drink kanyanga and smoke hemp, but I needed to change my behaviour. I obeyed from that moment on.

I resisted when the Major offered me drugs. I only got into drugs later, upon entering Rwanda so that I could endure the hard life. Our life as Mayibobo necessitates drug use. We can't live without it. Otherwise we would die *illico* (on the spot). We eat nothing apart from the leftovers in the garbage cans; we drink nothing apart from the gasoline that we suck through a cloth, and if we are lucky, we find some special glue that we use as an effective tranquilizer. By way of reward for my obedience, the Major's wife permitted me to eat the same food as her husband. This meal always consisted of manioc dough or mashed manioc with chicken or goat and, on rare occasions, pork.

Before, I had to be content with just broth occasionally, which was better than my snails. However, it is an ill wind that blows nobody any good; thanks to the food and motherly attention that our new mother doled out upon us, my little brother put on weight and was too heavy for me to carry. I didn't know what to do. I shared my anxiety with my new mother, my compatriot. To unload the burden from me, she took the child. It was she, from that day on, who carried my brother on her back while her two other children were entrusted to two soldiers, her husband's bodyguards. Later, my little brother would also be entrusted to a soldier.

I could never become a soldier because I have witnessed the blind obedience expected of them, especially the subordinates. Never would I carry a child who is not mine while the mother carries nothing. She would take only one gourd of boiled meat for her three children, my little brother included. She was spoiled, this woman. Another reason I wouldn't want to join the military is that they never tell the truth. The Major, for instance, though he was of Rwandan blood—even if he was disguised as a Zairian—was in connivance with the rebels. Though he was heading for Kin, his real mission was to put the brakes on the advancement of refugees approaching Kinshasa.

One good day, I surprised him as he was planning a military attack with another Zairian soldier from Bukavu. They were congratulating themselves for the work accomplished so far. This work consisted of stopping the refugees at Ikela so they couldn't avoid the rebels' murderous swords in the attack being prepared behind us. I understood, then and there, that they were all accomplices of the rebels.

I also understood why he had once sent three armed soldiers to kill four refugees who had stolen manioc from the field of a Zairian villager. The soldiers learned a good lesson that day. Usually it was they who looted everything—manioc, goats, chicken, pigs—so for them to accuse refugees of looting caused an uproar and resistance from furious refugees. When they arrived, threatening to kill the four refugees, all the other refugees present defended their compatriots. The soldiers accused them of being bandits. This was not true, and everyone knew it because everyone scoured the fields of the Zairians to stave off hunger since stomachs didn't know that the times had changed. The alleged robbers were tied to the gallows; they were to be shot.

When the signal was given to opening fire on them, all the refugees started to threw rocks at the soldiers. The soldiers dropped their weapons and took to their heels. The group of refugees was then attacked by a crowd of soldiers. The refugees, united as one, came to the aid of the little group who had been accused, each one with whatever weapon he could find: stick, machete, stone, whistle, etc. The soldiers resisted the order of the Major to fire on all the refugees without exception. No soldier would dare fire the first shot, and the combat ended in this way.

From the time of this incident, I understood that the Major had nothing good in mind for us. He wanted nothing but our death. The refugees decided to secretly distance themselves that very night. At this time, we arrived at the city of Ikela, very near the Tshuapa River which constituted a major obstacle for the refugees. The soldiers, with full knowledge of the facts, stopped us there. The real reason was to give the rebels time to organize and get to the river to massacre us there. The Zairian soldiers were the only ones allowed to occupy houses in the whole city. They had even confiscated all the *masua* (boats). We had been ordered to stop about one kilometre from the city, which also means from the river which flowed between the rebels and the Zairian soldiers as a protective shield. When I speak of *us*, I mean the refugees, even though my little brother and I were still with the Major's family in the same city, for I always shared the same cause with the refugees.

Some soldiers wanted to cross immediately, to get to Kinshasa as soon as possible, while others, in complicity with the rebels, wanted to prolong their stay. So a sharp dissension was created among the Zairian soldiers. As for the refugees, tired of waiting to cross the river, and aware of the next imminent attack—for news travels fast among refugees—they decided to pass secretly through the Zairian soldiers' camp. This venture was a success. They were careful to inform all Rwandans, even us who lived with the soldiers. We knew that these fleeing soldiers slept like the dead when they were drunk on kanyanga. And so it was that my little brother and I left our dear Mamma and her Major husband to join the refugee group.

However, we were not able to get across the Tsuapa River. It was impossible because the big masua had been confiscated by the soldiers. We took another road by way of Saint Paul's Parish, where no river crossed. Even if it was a longer and more dangerous route, the advantage was that it skirted the river. We left at about one in the morning. By 8 am we had covered about 15 km. We moved practically at a turtle's pace, walking two by two behind one another at the same pace, being sure not to make any noise. It was a technique we were well used to. We fell back on this strategy to pass through the ambushes set up by the rebels. This procedure helped us a lot, especially as we came out of the forest at Maniema, right near the route that joins Kisangani to the Lomami River. We had journeyed more than two weeks, moving as far away as possible from Kisangani, which had fallen into the hands of the rebels. We had plunged deeper than ever into the Equatorial Virgin Forest.

It's a shady forest where the only people were panning for gold and hunting for diamonds in the waters of the streams. A sieve was all that was needed. After a dangerous walk, we found ourselves near Kisangani, a city occupied by those who hunted us down like animals. We were trying to avoid these savages but had inadvertently approached them. There was a road nearby. Once we approached within 2 km of Kisangani, while we were still in the forest, we learned that the rebels were waiting for us to come out.

Once again, we had to resort to our Indian file method as we did near Kisangani. In fact, there, as we continued on, we exacted silence from everyone, even from the babies on the backs of their mothers or big brothers like me. The silence had to be absolute, so much so that once, when we were attacked by wasps in the forest for an hour no one dared open his or her mouth; to prevent the children from crying, mothers had to put hankies, scarves, or leaves from the trees in their mouths. My flesh had become hard like bone from the welts. I was miserable.

They were waiting for us as we came out of the forest exactly at the fork in the road going to Kisangani. We had to run to escape death. I ran like I was going for the gold in the 100 m, without even thinking about the baby who was on my back. The gold medal in this case was my nothing less than my life. Many lost their lives there. They were already so tired from the long journey and weakened by the wasp stings.

I remember a pretty young girl who fainted right at the end of that race. All the refugees abandoned her because they had to run for their own lives. It was each man for himself. She would certainly have been dead, had not a young man, perhaps smitten by her beauty or motivated by his own good will, stopped to give her a beneficial injection. He must have been a doctor, this young man. It was thanks to this injection that the young girl was able to stand up and wipe the foam from her mouth. Together they were able to walk away. From then on, they became inseparable friends. I couldn't run at the necessary speed, so I walked at a normal pace near them for a little while. I had no idea where the others had gone. So, I walked along with this last couple all the way to the Lomami River that I crossed with the Major and his family.

I don't know what became of this new couple. I hope that they are still alive. We had left that forest only a few minutes when we heard gunfire in the forest behind us. Without a doubt, they were killing those who, weary from the trip or sick, lagged behind us. This is how we escaped this death trap. The Zairian soldiers run before us and the last to embark were at Lomami River. Major was their commander. So, in the same way we left Ikela. If I were to look back on our trek from Ikela, I would say that we had avoided the river and our plan was successful even though there were some who were caught and killed. The plan was to begin moving after midnight, and the conditions were the same as when the Zairian soldiers had stopped us behind their line. There, we had used a light, only one torch for about one hundred people. So, anyone who would have seen us would believe in those fireflies that light up the night. So that we wouldn't get lost, the leader would use a rope.

Everyone was to hold onto this rope and keep pace. It was a fantastic method because the walk was rhythmic and didn't tire us too much. We left Ikela and as we were walking toward Bokungu, the Zairian soldiers awoke in the morning to find us gone. Fear overtook them. Panic-stricken, they hurried to try to get ahead of us. They had a boat. It would have been easy for them to go down to the waterway and to, once again, block the way before us. However, by the time they woke up, we were already far away. We had already broken rank to walk normally. Some had covered many kilometres since we were no longer restricted to the same pace. Another group, to which I belonged, chose to stop and prepare something to eat. We were caught by surprise. I was recognized by the Zairian soldiers. They stopped me straight away. Some of my companions were again successful in escaping, deeply penetrating the forest, very deeply. There, they met some rebels who were lying in waiting. Some were mercilessly massacred there while others were forced to backtrack only to be massacred at St. Paul's Parish in Ikela. I was given a lift back to the Major's family but a few hours later, I ran away again, to follow the tracks of the other refugees. I no longer feared anything.

KILLINGS AT MBANDAKA—
RWANDAN-STYLE MALICE

In the end, the Major, who had been waiting for the rebels, enlisted in the rebel army. I had guessed right. Hats off to me! At that time, there was no thought of lagging behind. Danger lay in wait for us. We had to fly to save our lives. We walked day and night without rest. Death was at our heels. If we were to escape it we had to move quickly. It was practically impossible for me to adjust to their pace, but, compelled to do so, I had to adapt so that death wouldn't catch me. If I lagged behind, I risked becoming prey for the cruel local population who was unhappy with the looting being done by the fugitive soldiers. I had no doubt that these rebels would capture me and either kill me or torture me. I knew that they were certainly capable of this since they had killed all of my family.

Food was scarce. Searches for food were sometimes carried out with violence and rationalized with casuistry. This massive displacement of refugees forced me to rediscover my old diet in a hurry. My little brother started to lose weight. After two weeks, we arrived at Bokungu but there was no way that we could live there. Everything had been pillaged and destroyed. Even Monsignor Njoku Mokobe, bishop of the diocese, spent day and night hiding in the *malenda* (bush).

We hurried on to reach Boende. The rebels had already arrived there. They were impatiently awaiting us, weapons in hand. The preparations for the massacre had been completed. They had arrived a long time beforehand, some on board the big boat, others by plane, and others still on foot, walking along with the refugees. It took only minutes to fly from Ikela to Boende, whereas it had taken us nearly a whole month on foot. A military boat could have arrived quickly too, because the river was navigable. The rebels were already there with all their military equipment. Once again, they massacred us mercilessly. They reasoned with the barrel of their guns, acted with malice, and were motivated by vengeance. Here, we were at the mercy of these heartless savages who had no mind or desire to reason humanely.

Fortunately, I was accustomed to their ways. I hid myself during the day and arranged my plans to walk with them at night. We had spent time together at Ingende. Unfortunately, the local population played a large part in these refugee massacres. They revealed our hiding places to our murderers. They didn't know what fate they themselves would later face. I am curious to know how much they were paid. The price of blood, I dare imagine because, when it comes to killing, our Rwandan soldiers or those of *Rwandan expression* as we like to designate those who hid their real Rwandan identity, it is done without pity. They are specialists in mass murder.

Ruki is a community situated on the shore of the Lomela River, a large river feeding into the Zaire River—pardon me, the *Congo* River because at this time the Mobutu government had been conquered and the name of Zaire had been replaced by the Democratic Republic of the Congo, the DRC. After arriving on foot, some of the rebels took boats, while the others returned to Boende by plane, then onward to Nselé. Other rebels, even more cruel than the last, preferred going to Mbandaka, this place that became a mass killing ground yet unrecognized by the International Community. Due to extreme fatigue, I was among those who still trailed along in the brush around the Lomela River. Several times I had to spend a whole day entirely immersed in water because soldiers were chasing us with hunting dogs. It was hell. We arrived at Mbandaka but not without difficulty. We came to realize how overpopulated Rwanda must have been, considering the many mass graves, as well as the bodies, unburied and unburned, scattered here and there in the bushes. We hid ourselves in the brush. The rebels, as well as the locals, were still hunting us down like dogs sniffing out wild game!

I don't know how, but by chance, I noticed a big snake near me, poised to bite me. I yelled for help, perhaps a little too loudly, because the rebels came to our aid. Still, I couldn't have refrained from yelling because the snake was so big and stared maliciously, threatening to spring on us. Once the snake was killed, the soldiers led us off to the slaughterhouse. It was a pauper's grave in which I saw corpses that were still moving.

My brother and I were lucky, for as chance had it, a few of the soldier in front of this common grave were discussing among themselves whether they should kill my little brother and me since we were the youngest in this delivery to the slaughterhouse. One of the rebels told us to run, without looking back, to the transit camp located in the direction to which he pointed. After several days of trial and error in choosing the road to take, because I was trying to avoid the road taken by the other refugees ahead of us, I arrived at Mbandaka, the transit camp. A miracle among so many others!

We had the good luck of not spending a lot of time at Mbandaka where the stench of unburied bodies mingled with the odour of drugs smoked by the soldiers and made our life unbearable. As well, every night, the rebels came to select refugees to offer to Hades, the god of the dead.

At Mbandaka, I was able to slip away with my little boy to the Congo River to try to cross it and reach Congo Brazzaville, just as other refugees had attempted at one time. Those upon whom luck had smiled did arrive on the other shore of the river. I told myself that there is no better man than the one that I met at Mbandaka!

I discovered three mass graves overflowing with the bodies of those who had been massacred in the previous few days. I was spared from these massacres in May 1997, the month of death for nearly every Rwandan and Burundian refugee who was still on Zairian soil. The rebels had formed a chain leaving only one way out, the waters of the river. The river was so immense that we couldn't see the other shore and swimming across it was impossible. Even so, some refugees did attempt this to escape the heinous death reserved for them if caught by the RAP's soldiers who had just become wolf. The waters of this river were so vast and imposing that they inspired fear and dread. Nevertheless, the river was our only possible exit since it was the solitary choice left to us by our torturers. These waters, hopefully our refuge, had been our hell several days before. If a refugee managed to get into a boat, safety was guaranteed. But it cost a fortune to buy passage to safety. There were many people, however, who were able to pass through the eye of the needle, escaping Congo Kinshasa for Congo Brazzaville on the other shore. There is truth in a Rwandan proverb: "*Ingona zirya bamwe abandi bambuka*" (Crocodiles tear some into shreds while others cross the river).

In Mbandaka, we had a second encounter with what seemed to be the end of our destiny after Mugunga and Inera of Bukavu. That day, I arrived at the river a little later, and at around 4 am I was awaiting a good will gesture from someone who would take me in his boat. This help never materialized. The fare to cross was 1,000 Zairian francs. I hoped to be able to negotiate with the Congolese, to try to appeal to their decency and common sense. That day, luck did not smile on us. When more than a hundred people came rushing in our direction, a boat soon appeared. A price of 1,000 Zairian francs was negotiated and agreed upon as passage for each person. I tried negotiating to pay half that much but without success. The boat left shore.

As it drifted away, tears ran down my cheeks. Heaven and earth had abandoned me. In the blink of an eye, all the difficult crossings I had overcome came to mind. The difficult locations I had crossed and especially the countless bodies that I had seen reassured me that my time had not yet come. I didn't know what to do. My life had just ended. I regretted not having been killed with my mother or my father because, without a doubt, at least they would always be there for me. The boat had gone but about 100 m when the rebels, like wind coming out of nowhere, attacked us. I trembled as I saw them approaching. One of them said to me, "*Rudi, nyumbani pumbafu!*" (Go home, imbecile!)

What home was he talking about? Maybe he meant Rwanda because it had been a long time since I had slept in a house. Maybe he thought that I was Congolese. This is not probable since he spoke to me in Swahili, a language no one speaks in this corner of Zaire. Everyone here speaks only Lingala. I definitely resembled the Zairians because of my filthiness. I resembled them because of my dirty rags, washed only in my sweat. Just a couple minutes later, I heard one of the rebels say "*faya*" (Fire)!

The noise that I heard from the guns made me fall to the ground where I lay motionless and unconscious for a while. When I came to, I crawled on my stomach, pulling with my elbows. It was unfortunate that I had to expose my little brother because he was on my back. I entered a bush and trembling, I watched the raking operation. The water had become red with blood.

Two military zodiacs arrived on the scene. I saw soldiers dive into the water. I didn't know what could possibly provoke them to dive into this bloodbath mixed with corpses. The river also held persons still alive, trying to swim to safety. Alas! Whoever tried to escape got a bullet that ended their attempt. It was horrible to watch. I was so traumatized by the sight of so many people killed that these images still drown my spirits. I spent a whole day without saying a word because I had to remain absolutely silent to avoid being discovered. My little brother, as well, does not speak very well. He had to spend his formative years in silence, a silence imposed upon him for his survival. What I lived through, that day, impregnated my entire life and changed my behaviour from that point on. To be totally honest, I have neither compassion nor pity for anyone.

I saw them scooping up bodies in nets, like fish. To this day, I can no longer eat fish. I believe that they have eaten human flesh and drunk the blood of Rwandans, whether in Rwanda during the Genocide when bodies had been thrown into the water or here, in this river from which nets filled with bodies were pulled with the help of boats. Then, they proceeded to cremate the bodies and throw the ashes into the water. I watched all this happen right before my eyes. When everyone had been burned, the soldiers withdrew into the city to hunt down those who might still be hiding in the forest. It was after they left that I made the wise decision to secretly return to the transit camp, the same one that I had deserted about a week before. Once I escaped from the soldiers who were trying to kill us, I found myself back in the transit camp of Mbandaka, the second one, possibly even the third transit camp because the first had been previously destroyed. Upon my arrival there, I spent three days in silence, not uttering a single word. I didn't know where I was. I had lost my mind. I didn't believe in God or the devil. I hated everyone.

Man had become a wolf, preying on his own species. Humans had acted too inhumanely toward compatriots. Since then, I have lost confidence in everyone, especially after these soldiers came again to kill us in this transit camp. After the destruction of the first transit camp by the RPA/ADFL soldiers, I escaped by the skin of my teeth. I found myself at the parish. I stayed there for several days, being treated like *mwana mboka* (a Zairian child).

After coming back to the second transit camp, I never stopped struggling with my troubled spirit until the day I fell ill and was transferred to the dispensary. I regained consciousness only after I was given fluids intravenously. I didn't know how I had gotten there. They offered to transfer us to Kigali, but I rejected their proposition. I expressed this by swaying my legs back and forth like I used to do to my mom to manifest my discontent. I was certain that Kigali would hold nothing but death. This is what I had heard from other refugees. No need to go to Kigali to die, for if I had to die, death was also present at Mbandaka.

I was sure that I had never put foot on Kigali soil. I had no idea what Kigali even looked like. While we were at the camp for displaced persons at Nyacyonga, I had longed to see this city that attracted children of my age. I no longer feared death, death that waited for me with open arms, death who had taken my dad, my mom, and my cousin Kayirangwa. I was still clinging to life. We had been informed that, at Kigali, the Inkotanyi were doing some serious killing, making no distinction between adults and children. They didn't tell any lies, these "made in Uganda" soldiers.

I knew how they killed because I had seen them in action when I was in the buffer zone of Kirambo with my family at Nyacyonga, the camp for misplaced persons, and then all over Zaire where I almost became their prey. I told myself that it wasn't only in Kigali-capital that death reigned as absolute master and had become omnipresent as long as there was a Rwandan refugee in proximity. That night, we heard terrible blows in the forest near the river. We were scared. A Congolese offered to be our nurse, not because he was good-willed, but in order to escape being murdered like the natives who had witnessed what had happened and could describe the macabre scene created by the torturers. These witnesses, an embarrassment to the soldiers, were eliminated during the night without the knowledge of the HCR.

This nurse frightened me and made me change my mind. He reminded me that the refugee camp at Mbandaka had been in existence for less than a month. Refugees had numbered in the hundreds of thousands. Every refugee who had been lucky enough to avoid being killed and to leave Ikela, Opala, Bokungu, Ingende, etc. had regrouped in this transit camp at Mbandaka.

One fine day, the bullies transformed this camp into a mass killing field as they were so accustomed to doing. They attacked from the east, opening up a corridor to the west, the direction of the river. This was the exact same strategy used beforehand at the Katale camp. At Rukwi, they had used a similar method, opening a path to the volcanoes. Accordingly, they used the same tried and true tactic. The river was ready to gobble us up alive. It served its purpose as they expected. It didn't let them down.

The transit camp at Mbandaka had been circled; the assailants had raided it in the afternoon. Those who still had any strength tried to run away. No matter in which direction they turned, they found soldiers waiting with their finger on the trigger to fire at them. Those who survived headed right out to the river. The soldiers continued their advance, killing everyone in their path. The refugees, who arrived at the shore of the river, having no option to turn back, had naturally continued on to the river. Did they believe that they could possibly do as Jesus did long ago when he walked on the water? Those who tried to swim across were chased by bullets. I got this information from an eyewitness who was hiding nearby, in the forest, at the time. At this point in time, the forest had not yet been the site of an attack. After fishing for bodies, incinerating the remains and throwing the ashes into the river, the operation changed shape. It was now time to comb the forest. Woe to those who had not escaped before the onset of this operation!

The ordeal lasted several days. Whenever I recall this story, my stomach is in knots and my legs feel as if they're tied together. I am no longer able to speak. Never before! Never before had fear seized me like that. Afterwards, I finally decided to die by going back to my ancestral country, Rwanda. After all, death pursued me everywhere. One could say that I moved with it. I wanted to go back to my homeland, even if I had no idea what lot awaited us. We could possibly even be lynched as soon as we put one foot on the soil of the country which, at one time, had been the country of our fathers. How were we to believe that these people who, at one time, came to kill us while we sought refuge, who pursued us relentlessly in a thousand places in Rwanda, would, this time, spare our lives? It was easy to make a decision such as this. It was a rather suicidal decision, believe me! Very early in the morning, when the doctor was making his rounds, I informed him that I wanted to return to Rwanda immediately. I got out of my sick bed on the spot, ready to leave at once. My little brother was asleep at my side. I woke him up and asked the doctor to stop the transfusions. I saw fear in his face as he leaned over me to calm me down. I told him curtly that I wanted to go back to my homeland. I had an appointment with death there. He would not consent to what I was asking him to do.

He didn't believe that I was serious. Since I had made up my mind, I took the catheter out myself in the presence of this doctor who tried, in vain, to stop me. Someone whispered into his ear that a plane would soon be going to Kisangani. Its purpose was to transport sick refugees. So, he gave me two bags of biscuits, a bottle of milk and placed me on a stretcher. I was driven to the airport at Mbandaka. It was very close by. They loaded me onto the plane. Once settled in, they restarted my fluids. A nurse was assigned to my care. She held my little brother in her arms. When I began screaming loudly, the nurse gave me an injection that made me immediately fall asleep. I didn't awake until we landed in Kisangani, which I mistakenly confused with Kigali.

I didn't know Kigali, the capital of my country. I had never been there, even though I had lived in the camp for displaced persons in Nyacyonga, a few kilometers from Kigali. I ascertained that it was a small city compared to Mbandaka. I was astounded to hear every-one speaking Kiswahili or Lingala. I was familiar with both of these languages. At Kisangani, only Lingala and French were spoken.

Everyone gave us exceptional care. I was surprised by that. I told myself that it was one way to trick us, by preventing us from being afraid, and consequently not trying to escape. I was experiencing the exact opposite of everything that we had been told about Kigali. This was not the Kigali I expected to find; Kigali that killed refugees coming back from exile. It was not the Kigali airport where death waited for me like a mother awaiting her son returning from afar. I had it in my head that I would be getting myself killed as soon as I got off the plane. It was almost incredible that we would be surrounded by such good care, only to be killed afterwards.

We have a proverb in our language that says, *"Ushaka kwica ubukombe arabwagaza"* (He who wants to kill the bull begins by stroking it), But I was too fascinated at the time to think of the proverb. Therefore, I drew the conclusion that I had been spared. I could've screamed at the top of my lungs: "Hurray! We are saved!"

Death it seemed had stayed back at Mbandaka. I thought of death as a person and so he couldn't be in more than one place at a time. I was enormously wrong. What followed contradicted my thinking. Death is immortal, invincible, untiring, and intolerable; it has no body other than those taken from our Rwandan brothers and sisters or those of Rwandan expression, the soldiers of the RPA. What a shame!

I kept on talking, not worrying about what those around me were saying since they treated me like a fool or a child suffering from trauma. They had deafened us by telling us that, as soon as we arrived in Kigali, we would be swiftly killed. But, in reality, they were taking too good care of us. I hadn't yet finished expressing that thought when I was loaded into an ambulance. After that, I have no idea how we left the Kisangani airport that I had mistaken for Kigali. How did we get to the transit camp at Kisangani? I have no idea.

When I awoke, I found myself in a hospital in the refugee transit camp at Kisangani. At my bedside was a nurse, but not the one who had accompanied me. Her name was Feza. She was Congolese[3] and spoke Swahili and a little Kinyarwanda. I remember the first words she said to me when I came to: "*Komera sha, petit!*" (Be strong, don't worry, my little one!)

"*Turi i Kigali?*" (Have we arrived at Kigali?), I asked her right away.

"No, not at Kigali but at Kisangani," she calmly and affectionately replied.

In the blink of an eye, I saw everything that we had lived through; the massacres, the fatigue, the hunger, etc. to get to Kisangani. Fear paralysed me.

My heartbeat accelerated. I was sweating like someone thrown into an oven. The nurse called in the doctor. He took my pulse and checked my heart and lungs. He advised that I be carefully monitored. He said that I was to be wiped down with cold cloths and to continue the treatment for some time. I could hear them speaking. I didn't want to respond to the infantile questions they were asking me. How should I answer a question like this: "Where are your parents?"

I was angry at them. I was always angry with anyone who asked me where my parents were and how they were killed. It's like they thrust a sword into my heart already streaming blood. Once the doctor had gone, I asked nurse Feza if we were in Kigali. I could sense that she was reticent to answer so I spoke first and said: "When are you going to kill us?"

She replied kindly and fondly: "Don't be afraid of anything. We are not killers, we are caregivers."

Do you think that I believed her? Not for a minute! A patient in the next bed interrupted, speaking in Kinyarwanda, my native tongue. He reassured me that we were indeed in Kisangani, not Kigali. He said, in a voice barely audible because of the critical state of his health: "*Erega mwana turi i Kisangani. Bya Bishuga ntabiri*

---

3   Now that Kabila Joseph had chased away Maréchal Mobutu, the ex-President of Zaire and had changed the name of the country, the people were called Congolese and the country rebaptized Democratic Republic of Congo (DRC), now we will use the term of Congolese to refer to the people of DRC; Congo to refer to the country, the former Zaire.

hano. Dufite hano twe umutekano." (We are in Kisangani. The blood-thirsty wolves are no longer here. We are safe here.)

I had been so afraid to come to Kigali where I believed that death ruled as dictator. At once, I sat up to try to make sense of reality. I saw men and women battered to the bone. All that could be identified were eyes bulging out of big heads. Everyone had become like tadpoles; the size of their heads was no longer proportional to the rest of their bodies which had been reduced to bones without muscles. They were so gaunt that they needed the help of a nurse to stand up. I found that I felt sturdier. Fear continued to betray me. I felt like I was in a concentration camp where everyone was starving to death. I was mistaken. There was an abundance of food. Two pretty women came in to distribute milk to the patients. Everyone was given a large glassful. I refused to drink it, for I thought that it had been poisoned.

Yes, I still was not convinced that I wasn't in Kigali. I didn't tell them that these were my reasons for not drinking it. A minute later, a young man whose stature was typical Congolese, came in with cookies. He loved to sing and whistle. He gave five cookies to each person. He gave me ten. I was with my little brother, so I got twice as many as the others. I love cookies so much that I couldn't pass them up. I took a few and started eating them. I had gotten into the habit of taking one from each end of the stack and throwing them out the window. I told myself that they had put poison either on the top one or under the bottom one. I believed that they had poisoned only those two.

Everyone's eyes stared at me, but no one dared to ask me what I was doing. They were all astonished at the hearty appetite with which I ate those cookies since they thought me to be seriously ill. Another astonishing thing was that I was tossing away one cookie from the top and one from the bottom. The young man who was distributing the cookies was so happy that I was finally eating that he gave me ten more. Inwardly, I told myself that such generosity would not go unpunished. He was probably trying to fatten me up so I'd be plump for the killing. I had to mistrust any gifts that came my way!

The nurse looked affectionately and compassionately at my little brother and me in a way that reminded me of the Major's wife. She took a little cup of my milk. She took a sip of it then offered me the rest which I accepted. She acted like this according to our culture: if someone offers you something to eat or drink, he would first take a small amount and consume it in your presence to prove that it had not been poisoned. These people knew about our culture, and when I threw out two cookies, one from the top and one from the bottom, they understood what I was doing since the young man who had offered them didn't eat those two that I threw away. So, the woman who offered me milk had understood my gesture of throwing away the cookies. I couldn't imagine that a woman acting so tenderly toward us, would give us poison. I considered her to be very kind to have acted so. When I had finished drinking the milk, she hugged me tightly as if to congratulate me. Finally she said to me: *"Urakoze cyane."* (Thank you very much.)

From that day on, she became like my mother to me. She replaced my mother whom I had lost in the forest. My heart was soothed. From then on, whatever she gave me, I ate with gusto. At Kisangani I gained weight, quite a bit actually. I had become a big "jojo".

Since I had neither parents nor any other adult person with me and I was under the age of 18, we were taken in by the ENA (Agency for Unaccompanied Children). They gave us soap, clothes, and food in sufficient quantity and at regular hours. As well, they would bathe us—one thing I had forgotten about a long time ago. In short, we were spoiled. The forest had made me a specialist in guerrilla tactics, so I could no longer sleep peacefully in a closed camp. They loved to speak Swahili to me. I avoided spending the night in the dormitory with the other children. No, they were not adept in the art of soldiering. A true commando, such as myself, would never spend the night in a house. As long as war raged, I had to be on my guard. One never knew because evil ones never took a break.

The enemy was always on watch and on the lookout for an opportunity to wipe us off the face of the earth. Why us?

Every time the dormitory supervisor retired for the night, I too, withdrew after him, to spend the night in the bushes, an activity I had found to be very beneficial. The brush had saved my life on several occasions. I headed for a spot near the latrines, not far from the APROSOMIR, a Congolese ONG that worked with another one named EUB. During the night, while the refugees slept, I could get updated on everything that was going on at the transit camp. It was terrible. It was God who allowed the refugees to stay asleep, I swear!

Prostitution was rampant between 10 pm and midnight. The soldiers, as well as the rebels, came into the camp during the night: this was not allowed in other places. They took refugee girls. I don't know how they chose them. The same girls always followed them. They were probably selected by the Zairian workers at the camp. It was really a big brothel! These girls screamed a lot. In the end, they were paid in *"maheshi"* (Zairian money) that was worthless. All of this transpired not far from me. I paid attention to all that they were doing, like a journalist who didn't want to miss a single detail. I would sleep only after they had gone. Curiously, all these soldiers spoke Kinyarwanda. They looked a lot like Rwandans. Through them, I learned how Kisangani and Kasese, had been transformed into a mass refugee killing field because I heard them ask the girls how they had managed to survive there. They sometimes asked their forgiveness. From the bottom of their hearts? I don't know. Also, I got to know which refugees in the camp were designated to be the next victims. I did warn them, even if they didn't want to believe me.

My covert operation also allowed me to discover a plot that was being drafted against the refugees. Since I was afraid of reliving what I had experienced in Mbandaka, I made the decision to commit suicide by choosing to return to Rwanda. I dreaded Kigali, but I dreaded Kisangani even more, after having witnessed the carnage there. I had seen many bodies since Tingi-Tingi and before that at the Oso River and the refugee camp at Amisi. There had been massacres at Kisangani-city, along the road at Kilometre 82, Kilometre 49, Kilometre 52 of Kisangani as well as the famous Kasesa where refugees were mercilessly massacred in a systematic fashion and their bodies burned.

Death swallowed up so many. I believed that death must have been sated by all this human flesh, but I was mistaken. Actually some refugees, with much difficulty, had crossed the Lualaba River, the first big stream to the east of the Zaire River. Those who tried to spend the night on the shore of this river, paid the price with their blood. They were attacked and killed that same night. The small number who survived hid in the forest. There, they were hunted down by their executioners, aided by some of the local population. These poor peasants, armed with spears and arrows and guided by hunting dogs, had crisscrossed all through the forest. But, at that time, the primary intention of the pursuers was not to kill, but rather to seek out all the refugees and to regroup them at Kisangani. Once assembled, these refugees would be making their way to Rwanda under the guise of the Voluntary Repatriation of Refugees, which is what they said of all the refugees who re-entered Rwanda, regardless of the conditions surrounding their repatriation, even those who came back with arms and legs bound together from Gabon! It wasn't all that voluntary. In the end, I too, took the road to Rwanda.

Once I arrived in Rwanda, I headed directly to what had been our house and our land in the northern part of the country in the prefecture of Ruhengeri. The UNHCR trucks drove us to our original communities. I found only new faces there. The people who now occupied our home and taken over our family's goods, all came from Uganda, the neighbouring country in the north. It was very close by. When they learned that we were still alive, they vowed to kill me. Thankfully, they didn't know who I was. I had grown up so much. Our former neighbours no longer recognized me either. They had no knowledge of my little brother.

They expressed it this way: We don't want any of these Interahamwe who left the country after having killed all the Tutsi. We will inflict the same fate upon them as those killed in 1994. This was, evidently, far from the truth. They confused—and continue to confuse—all Hutus for Interahamwe. Besides, at the time of the Genocide, I was too young to kill the Tutsi. As for my little brother, he was not yet born. Why, then, treat him like an Interahamwe that he never even knew! When the other villagers reasoned with them, pointing out that we were but little children, they kept their dirty plan to themselves: kill the former owners and seize their goods. Instead of listening to former owners, they threatened to treat them like Interahamwe which would entail being imprisoned or killed without apology as they believed should be done to every captured Interahamwe. My neighbours continued to insist that it was not possible for me, a child of five, to have killed a child of my age or have yelled out against a Tutsi who was trying to escape, and that my little brother would have acted accordingly.

The situation became too tense and threatened our survival, so I decided to go to Kigali about 80 km to the south. I had learned that there were children who lived there, roaming the streets, "street kids" commonly called *Mayibobo*. I didn't know any of them but this resolution was compelling. In Kigali, the children lived in the streets where anonymity was such that no one would dare to accuse them of committing Genocide or of being Interahamwe just to seize the goods that the family had left to them. With the Mayibobo, I would live like a parasite, like the birds for sure, but at least I would live far from the hateful looks triggered by desire for my family's property.

Since that day, I have lived at the expense of the streets of Kigali. They offer us hospitality, one thing humans have refused us. When I arrived at the bus station at Nyabugogo, I didn't know where to go. I decided to go to the left as I was accustomed to doing every time I came to a crossroads. This is how I made my way to downtown Kigali where I met children whose living conditions were about to become mine. They welcomed us unconditionally and integrated us into their organizations. And so, we became Mayibobo for all time. The life of a Mayibobo is a life that is *powa sana* (right, correct). We live freely. Long live freedom! No one invents stories to cause us to perish. We need neither beds for sleeping nor homes for the night nor blankets to protect us from the cold. We spend the nights under bridges, on the roofs of homes, in the streets, in dumpsters, wherever! Dumpsters serve as beds and houses and their rubbish keeps us nourished. We often sleep under the stars or on the floor of vehicles. I can sleep at any hour of the day, and I can allow myself a siesta. I live like a king and my kingdom is not of this world, but of the avian world, since I live perched atop the high-rises of Kigali. Everyone is my friend; everyone is my enemy. I trust no one because humanity has become fundamentally inhumane. "I don't have any religion" to mean that I am of no religious persuasion, a common expression in Kinyarwanda which meant that one is carefree and can change affiliation from one moment to another. I do not fear the future. I live from day to day. I have no projects or plans. I do whatever comes to mind. I have no compassion for anyone. I have no more tears or remorse for what I have done. Living is of no importance to me. I am already a corpse who doesn't know it. I fear the past because it took everything from me and refused me everything. I hate the future that doesn't want to welcome me. Has God abandoned me, I who am baptized and who carry the baptismal name *Mayibobo* (Street Kid)?

People trying to make a living selling small items. This was a local market.

What do you think would be the future of this abandoned boy?

We are receiving subsidies to live on. We had to live
like this for almost two years. What a shame!

This is the site Q. It is bordered by a forest
where many of us lost our lives.

This is a refugee camp. These are the houses we lived in. We named
them "bulende" (armoured military car) referring to what the
soldiers used to destroys our houses while we were in Rwanda.

These are street kids sharing what they had stolen.

These were children whose parents were killed during the genocide against the Tutsi or by RPF soldiers. The oldest took care of the young ones. Do you think he would be able to go to school?

These children now form a new family without any parents or adult to take care of them. What hope do you think they have for their lives?

PART TWO

MAYIBOBO, MIRROR OF THE RWANDAN SOCIETY

The testimony of these two children, Mbazende and Ntazina, condemned to live on the streets of Kigali following the death of their parents in the forests of Zaire in 1996, brings to light one of the causes of the social phenomenon commonly referred to as "Mayibobo Street Kids". This causal relationship is almost forgotten by those who are trying to find a solution to the problem. Certain children are victims of the recent history of Rwanda—since war began on October 1, 1990, the date the RPF attacked Rwanda from Uganda in the north. Many parents were killed, leaving behind numerous orphans who must support the family themselves. For the first time in Rwandan history, a multitude of children took to the streets of the capital city, Kigali.

We never saw children living in the streets before this war. This is a point that should not be forgotten. This phenomenon is inherent to the wars that were fought in our country. The Mayibobo slogan is *"Wamfunguriye!"* (Give me something to eat!) They came from camps at Rutongo, specifically Nyacyonga and others that were set up for people displaced; the term "displaced persons due to war" was applied to Rwandans who abandoned their homes, their lands, and their goods to flee from the killings of RPF and its army RPA. These displaced persons were fleeing from the advancing RPF.

Nearly all the children had originally lived in the Communes—now known as districts or municipalities—of the Province of Byumba, formerly the Prefectures of Byumba. All of those bordering on Uganda were affected. It also included the municipality of Mutura and Rwerere in Gisenyi as well as the municipalities of Tare and Rushashi in rural Kigali. The children, orphaned by the war, dashed into the streets, seeking help to survive. Sadly, instead of receiving help, they were often sent away empty-handed, or were the recipients of insults such as, "Go ask Kinani for help; he is responsible for bringing this wretched war upon us." Kinani was a nickname, given by the opposition, to President Habyarimana a few months before the Genocide to harm his good reputation.

So, Rwanda still suffers today from this disease called "Mayibobo Street Kids". As of yet, no vaccine or medication has been found to combat it. Despite trials of several medications, the disease continues to be resistant, despite the efforts of researchers and caregivers. Why this resistance? Why the failure?

It seems to me that they have gone too quickly to treatments without considering an analysis of the causes of this phenomenon. Cleaning up the city of Kigali, the location frequented by most of these helpless souls, has been the priority. These rejected beings, outcast from the society that they mirror, are still a problem. The treatments to date have addressed neither the symptom nor the causes and, therefore, have failed. The overdosing of this treatment not only failed to destroy the Mayibobo, it also did not address the causal agent, which is to say Rwandan Society itself.

When it was decided to drive these children far from the city of Kigali to Gikongoro, for example, or to the island of Iwawa on Lake Kivu, in preparation for the grand reunion of NEPAD at Kigali, it was not a solution that took into account the child and what caused him to roam the streets in the first place. The city of Kigali had to be cleaned of its *filth*, certainly, but man is not a piece of garbage that can be thrown away like that. A hypo-dosage was also considered in the treatment. I call hypo-dosage the solution that consisted of leaving the child to his own devices. It begs the question, was no one concerned with this type of child and whether he lived or not? Whether these children were there or not, or existed at all, meant the same thing. Whether these children would grow up or not; eat or not; were questions of no importance in a country far more focused on Advanced Technology.

Lastly, there is the risk of familiarization with the medicines doled out and the body's tolerance. This devalues the child to the point that he confuses himself with that with which he gorges himself, the rotting food from the garbage. What was needed was an aggressive campaign against this phenomenon, similar to the fight against AIDS or the use of plastic bags throughout the whole country where, from the youngest to the oldest Rwandan people, all of us together, were summoned to pick up these bags and burn them once and for all.

Even though there were multiple efforts to find a solution to this question, which is in and of itself complex, there is still much to do because everything we contemplate must benefit the children and take into consideration their pain. The consensus is that we did not put forth the necessary effort, acting as if the child's needs should always be the last to be served. This problematic issue requires the attention of every person concerned with the future of our Rwandan society, post-Genocide. This collaboration must encompass all sectors, from sociologist to anthropologist, from the politician to the religious and extend to all people. These children need the kind of affection that emanates from someone who knows how to open their hearts as would a mother or father or sister or brother. It is equally important that they be integrated into society rather than creating a ghetto or a microcosm where the risk is that the child will lock himself in forever. Furthermore, the government's policy on social affairs must protect the most vulnerable: children, indigents, homeless, and the starving who are so numerous in and around Kigali. The problem of mothers who, very early in the morning, go to downtown Kigali to beg in the streets and go back home at night, necessitates a solution adapted to their needs. One possible solution would be to foster small businesses, an avenue that the State seems to discourage.

If the principle of *education for all* were effectively extended to everyone, the number of street kids would possibly diminish, for *all* must be understood to include every child of elementary school age whose education should be free. In order to do this the State should adjust the teachers' salaries to be in line with the exorbitant prices charged in the country's markets. It's very regrettable that the salary of these intellectuals, upon whom the transmission of knowledge depends, cannot even allow them to buy sugar for their tea or coffee. To survive, they must ask the children to pay them a premium. Many children take to the streets because their parents cannot afford to pay the tuition. Poverty is growing day by day. The unemployment rate is higher than ever. The small payment called "serum" no longer covers essential needs for a few lucky Rwandan who get jobs. In contrast, the President is buying for his use, two Bombardier Jets and spending nights in luxurious hotels for $20,000 a night while visiting the USA. What corruption! Where is true patriotism? The consequences?

Many people are killed because they want to denounce this injustice. Many people are sent to jail because they want to talk about this dirty little secret—a President who has been given the image of a good leader in order to be awarded a prize for so-called *good governance*! Many children, because of poverty, have no choice but resorting to live on the streets. Often, they are encouraged to do so by their parents.

AN AGGRAVATING SITUATION
THE MASSACRES OF THE HUTU AND THE GENOCIDE OF THE TUTSI

The Genocide and the massacres only increased the number of street kids. Their parents and relatives had just been viciously killed. Some children were the sole survivors from a large family of 8, 10 or more children. It's a very serious and unimaginable situation. They were confronted with a new familial situation once they found themselves deprived of their parents and relatives, who had always provided for all their needs. The war provoked a grave injustice. The children, deprived of all assistance and help, must nevertheless feed themselves as well as other children in their charge. How are they to accomplish this?

What are they to eat? They have nothing. They wander in the streets of Kigali asking any passerby for food. From this activity come the slogans so often chanted in the streets, *"papa wamfun-guriye"* (Dad, have pity on me, give me something to eat); *"papayi wampaye agaceri"* (Daddy, give me a small coin) or *"mamayi, wampaye agaceri"* (Mommy, give me a small coin); *"bosi we wamfun-guriye"* (Boss, give me something to eat); or again, *"mukuru wanjye wampaye agaceri"* (Big brother, give me some money).

These powerless children witnessed the macabre death of their loved ones. There's something to cause fear! They're living with a time bomb. Everything that they passively witnessed is stored in their subconscious. It is actively repressed, far from the scope of consciousness, and persists because it surpasses all understanding. Just as the water table searches for a crevice in which to rise up again, these memories, repressed into their subconscious, seek an outlet. Unconsciously, this influences their behaviour. Some children become mentally depressed, insane, traumatized, delinquent or future tyrants. They have lost their family; as specialists like Richard Cloutier and Andre Renaud say: "The family is called to fulfil the bio-psycho-social functions on behalf of the child, while at the same time, fulfilling functions that assure the survival of the society in which it is inscribed as the fundamental cell." (Psychology de l'enfant, Gaëtan Morin éditeur, Montréal, 1990, p. 612). The children will manage, by trying to fulfil the functions that this family no longer can because it is dislocated. This is not without danger from the child's point of view as well as for all of society.

I had the opportunity to live with children such as these. They ranged in age from 4 to 18 years. The behaviour of those aged 6 to 13 had a very special characteristic. They were always expecting the worst. They were children who had no regard for anything. They were impervious to reprimands, corrections, and chastisements. When they fight amongst themselves, they use any weapon available: knives, stones, broken glass, etc.

This age, according to child psychologists, is a transitional stage where children are gradually freeing themselves from their emotional dependence on parents and family to develop friendly relationships with others. The child is training himself or herself how to love others. The automatic, passive love the child felt when surrounded by caring and protective parents begins to diminish because a longer period of time is spent separated from them. They will learn the new rules and values that govern the group to which she or he now belongs. He learns to respect them. The child is obliged to come to terms with the new milieu and at the same time understand it and make it his or her own. In a word, he or she evaluates everything, based somewhat on what was learned from parents in the past. And so, our street children, especially the age group with which we are now concerned, were born or grew up in an ambiance of war with incredible, unheard of violence, Genocide, massacres and worse yet, they are now surrounded by bandits, prostitutes and garbage cans. They did not receive a solid foundation upon which they could base their discoveries. They have to come up with models upon which they can evaluate their criminal dealings. It's extremely regrettable! Rwandan society will have to pay the price.

Normally, the children of this age group are active, curious, fearless, and inventive. To be so, they need someone they can trust who will watch over them without stifling their ingenuity, imagination, and inventiveness. This is the role that an educator should play, taking time to explain and bring to light safety rules and the danger of always following one's inclinations. If a child understands the reasons for such things, he or she would readily keep them in mind. Sadly, the children of whom we are speaking have neither parents nor educators. In the event that the child had one, the parent or educator would know how to react to a child whose traumatism triggers an awakening of old wounds caused by life experiences, such as war. Does not the Latin proverb say, *"Medice, cura te ipsum!"* (Healer, heal thyself).

"The most beautiful girl in the world can only give what she has," echoes another French proverb. This age group is known for its hearty appetite. But what will they eat, these children whose life depends on the generosity of the garbage cans?

What Is Permissible For the Cow Is Not So For the Dog[4]

I don't want to insinuate anything here. It's just that, among the street kids, some are traumatized and feel authorized and entitled to outwardly manifest their feelings, while others only internalize them even more because of an attitude of uncertainty. A child in this latter category explained to me what, in their jargon, they call the snail approach, *"Tagitiki y'ikinyamujongo."* It is similar to the Latin expression *"Audi, vide, tace, si vis vivere."* (Listen, look, be quiet if you want to live). A snail is an invertebrate whose body is housed in a sort of shell. It doesn't come out of its shell until its tentacles or antennae have assured its safety on the outside. In other words, it scrutinizes the environment using its tentacles and, once assured that there is no danger, it moves its body almost totally out of the shell. It will never come out unless assured that it is safe.

These street kids are not the only ones in the country who will not speak unless they are 100% sure of their surroundings. Actually, in Kigali, it is often said that, of three people who are gathered together in Rwanda, two are of the Intelligence Branch. Consequently, many people won't dare to show their distress since, *"Imfubyi ibaga yotsa."* (The orphan is recognized by his resourcefulness, by the way he does not cry out even if he's being stepped on, by his ability to maintain silence because he doesn't have the right to cry out loud). Many children, especially those whose parents are labeled—rightly or wrongly—as genocidal, feel as though they are strangers in their homeland. If they are here, it's because of a favour, not a right. This privilege can be retracted from one minute to the next. Living is a gift. And we do not exact a gift. We receive it, only when it is offered to us. What good would it do to cry aloud, when screaming is only a reminder that you are an undesirable, one who is intrinsically worthless. They practice absolute silence. To survive, these children resorted to the rubbish bins unless they were being chased away by the police.

---

4   − A proverb in our language says, "Imbwa yigannye inka kunnya mu rugo irabizira" (A dog took the liberty of defecating on the farm and he was beaten). This is also what the Latin version attempted to express in these words: *"Licet iovi, non licet ignovi"* (What is permitted to the cow is not permissible for the dog).

How did I come into contact with them? How did they finally agree to allow me to penetrate their double-locked microcosm? I made myself small like them and went down to the streets where they lived. I played with the children to keep them occupied. My mission was to raise their morale and to instill in them some value as a human who is created in the image and likeness of God. Yes, man has value and dignity. In other words, a human being is "a person", a word used to emphasize the dimension of dignity and value, as philosophers say, in regard to personhood and personality development. I wanted to realign their behaviour, to bring them from a state of barbarism, even savagery, to the point of being integrated into society. I didn't want them to continue living on the margins of Rwandan society. I thought this would be an easy undertaking. I didn't realize that these children, while living isolated from society, but guided by the instincts of self-preservation and survival, had developed another defence mechanism. It is certainly true that all living beings who are threatened by extinction develop this instinct. And so, apparently, these sad children are no different from other children of their age, except that they know how to camouflage their problems, whereas others talk about their problems to those who are able to listen to them and to understand, namely parents and relatives. These children are unoccupied and tend to like solitude. They would curl up timidly in a corner and attack the others.

I found this behaviour strange since children of this age are usually dynamic, ingenious, inventive, and creative. When we approached them, they had a tendency to flee. We didn't succeed in gaining their trust because nothing seemed to attract them. They live in an interior world of their own to such a degree that no one has the right to enter it. They are afraid of adults or they hate them because of what they have made them suffer. In order to gain their confidence, I became their friend and a child like them. When I ascertained that they were more or less attracted to the bravery theme, I cried out to myself, like Archimedes, "Eureka! I've found it!"

To begin with, I liked to ask them to draw anything of their choice for me. Then, in explaining their drawings, they all described to me scenes showing human beings inhumanely killing other human beings. While doing so, they expressed fear and it wasn't rare that they hugged me tightly as if they were hiding from something. Some of them cried while vehemently saying, "I'll kill them too!"

CATEGORIES OF THESE STREET KIDS

These are the categories of children found in the streets of Kigali. Each one, by their drawings, allowed me to enter into the depths of their life. All of the names we are going to use were also given to adults based on the fact that they lived in the country before, during, or after the Genocide of 1994. So *Sopecya* refers to people who were in Rwanda and remain there even after the Genocide. Those who entered Rwanda from Zaire where they were in exile for long time were called *Dubaï* or *Banyamulenge*; they were all of the Tutsi. Those who were Hutu who left Rwanda after the Genocide and came back from Zaire were called *Tingi-Tingi*. The ancient Rwandan refugees who came back from Burundi were *GP*, those from Tanzania were *TZ*, and those ancient refugees who came back from Uganda were known as *Sagya*—the majorities were of the families of soldiers and politicians who lead Rwanda at that time.

All children who had been in exile in Zaire since 1994 were designated as Tingi-Tingi. They indistinctly carried this name, cliché, or disparagement even if they had never been to Tingi-Tingi. In general, those who were designated as Tingi-Tingi were at the same time assumed to be Interahamwe. This was a generalization that aimed to reduce them to silence.

The street kids, so designated, had drawn pictures that were difficult to decipher; pictures of planes dropping bombs on weak fugitives who were begging their forgiveness. Some children drew a huge crowd gathered on a plain, holding each other and positioned in the shape of a cross. These Tingi-Tingi fit into several categories: those who moved directly from Goma to Rwanda, and those who had to spend several days in the dark, wild forests of the Congo before being forced to repatriate to Rwanda. In the last category were those who had to travel many, many kilometers in the heart of

Zaire. They risked being devoured by beasts in the Equatorial Forest or being killed by human predators. They spent several months in the hope of a second chance of living, for they were targets for killing, often lost, succumbing to fatigue, hunger, and drowning. These children were also at risk of being abandoned by their parents and relatives, and of being permanently separated from their families. Some parents did rid themselves of their children so that they could run more quickly, once freed of the burden these children represented. I interpreted this cross to represent the one they would have erected on the graves of their loved ones who they were unable to bury. Actually, in Rwanda, we do put up a cross on the grave of our loved ones and it is the next of kin who plants it. It said that the majority of them on their run had covered more than 13,000 km on foot. Even if this figure were exact, one would have to add the multiple circling and tours they made in the forest when lost and searching for right road; this was a fight for survival because whoever, unfortunately, lagged behind the others were captured and beheaded or lynched by the assailants, the Rwandan RPA soldiers who were thirsty for Hutu refugee blood.

The Sopecya are those who resisted but were prevented from leaving the country when everyone was abandoning Rwanda for bordering countries. The children from this group tended to draw empty caskets. They were also of three sub-categories: those who drew an empty casket, those who drew people consumed by grief and alienated from the group, and those children who drew people in hiding. Of this last category, a little 8 year old girl drew a scene where another child, a little boy, was begging forgiveness saying, "*Mbabarira we; sinzongera kwitwa umututsi!*" (Forgive me; don't kill me. I'll never again call myself a Tutsi). He was of course innocent. He doesn't really know what is going on. He only knows that being a Tutsi was a mistake like stealing cookies from your mother's table. To kill such an innocent child is worse than Genocide—even though there are no degrees in matters of such inhumanity.

By examining the themes of their drawings, other sub-groups were revealed: orphans of the Genocide. They were children whose parents, brothers and sisters had been savagely killed simply for being Tutsi. Among them were those who had been recovered by extended family members, those who were able to escape for good, and those who came back from Zaire and the other countries immediately after the military victory of the RPF. They had been so mistreated that they preferred to wander in the streets. There at least, they felt free and didn't have to subject themselves to the lack of understanding by those who were not their relatives. There were children who had been raised by surrogate families. Very often, they did not feel comfortable with them. In most cases, we could say there was transplant rejection. The families who welcomed children into their homes expected advantages and monetary gain from the State, ONG, churches, or FARG (Funds for Genocide Survivors), but they had been deceived. Some foster families hoped to possibly get some remuneration from a member of the child's family who was in the West and, according to the family, would eventually send support money. These disappointed families sent the children back to the orphanage as swiftly as they had previously pulled them out. These children were threatened and mistreated so much that they decided to abandon these orphanages. They headed for the streets far away. There were also some who had been sent back to the orphanage once the foster family realized that they were of another ethnicity.

Finally, in another sub-group were the children whose parents had been killed by the RPA. The majority of this last group had lost their loved ones in the prefecture of Byumba. Yes, in the same city of Byumba, where the same army assembled the Hutu population for a meeting and its soldiers had circled those gathered together and massacred all of them with automatic weapons and grenades. Others were killed following a selective draw, targeting solely the Hutu from the Commune of Giti where the Hutu population of Kigali had been driven by the RPA. Many Hutu were executed there even if the government of Kigali still affirms today that no one was killed in this municipality—unless they considered the Hutu to no longer be human persons. The Fratri Makanaki, Father Cyrille, is the only survivor of the seminarians and priests from the minor seminary of Rwesero (Byumba) where 11 priests and seminarians were atrociously killed by the RPA on April 21, 1994; his testimony contradicts the statements of the government whose hands are stained with the blood. This is how the number of Hutu killed by that army grew since the war of October 1990.

Similarly, others went out to harvest the rice or unload food supplies and to date have simply not returned. "Harvesting rice or beans" –or– "going to unload trucks of food supplies" were euphemisms used by the RPA to select the Hutus—mostly males—that they planned to execute far away from the rest of the assembled population. For example, in the Commune of Giti, there would otherwise be a lot of human remains were the bodies of the Hutus massacred by the RPA assembled in one place, despite the fact that the Army and their politicians said that there were no killings in this Commune—perhaps their definition of killing refers only to the murder of Tutsi but not of the Hutu by RPA!

The soldiers of the RPA employed multiple tricks during the massacres of the Hutu within the country. They would convene large groups for a meeting during which everyone present was executed with heavy artillery. Smaller groups might meet with a specific torture named Akandoyi that ended with a blow to the head with a worn-down hoe. This method of torture consisted of tying the victim's hands and legs together behind their back. Thus, the body would form an strained arc. All the assailant had to do was strike the chest with any object to split the thoracic cage into two parts, thereby splitting the victim in half.

Sometimes the RPA soldiers would attack camps for displaced persons to exterminate the population. This was the case in the massacres at the camp of Kibeho during which tens of hundreds (8000 victims would say Terry Pickard in Camp de Kibeho, Rwanda avril 1995, crimes FPR Kibeho; or 25000 victims according to CNN in the news of April 17-20) perished by the sword of the RPA which operated under the auspices of the MINUAR II, soldiers who represented the ONU in Rwanda.

The family could also be at the root of the juvenile delinquency of the Sopecya. Actually, some children fled from family poverty or because of disagreements among family members. Several children chose to distance themselves from the family home where there was no harmony among its members. Every time the father came home, he abused his wife in the presence of the children. Sometimes they were forced to hide from their father who had become like a lion. Since it is in the nature of the child to always want to help his or her mother, but not yet able to, the child prefers to leave the paternal home rather than to passively witness the tortures and harassment of the father against the mother. This type of Mayibobo valued training in the martial arts in the hopes of, one day, avenging their unhappy mothers. In this group, the girls vowed not to marry for fear of the possibility of being subjected to the same treatment as their mothers. As we explore the origins of these juvenile delinquents, among the Sopecya, we could also include the category of those who, on a whim, decided to distance themselves from their family. The reason for their flight is to be found elsewhere.

The category of the Dubai included the children whose parents were killed in Zaire and headed for safety in Rwanda. They became orphans as a result of the operation called *Kimya* under Marshal Mobutu, the President of Zaire at the time. His soldiers were deployed to Masisi where they killed all the Tutsi. Since Tutsi families living in Masisi raised a lot of livestock, these children sometimes drew pictures of soldiers eating human flesh alongside the beef from their cattle. They also drew straw houses burning down. It was not uncommon to see drawings depicting herds of abandoned cattle without shepherds. Sometimes their sketches showed *inkongoro zirimo ubusa* (empty milk jugs) to express that they had not taken any milk with them even though milk had flowed like a stream when they were at Masisi.

The category of the Banyamulenge were children who had also grown up in Zaire but whose ancestors were Mulenge. They had been chased from Zaire, originating mostly from Kamanyola and Uvira. They liked to call the others *Panya* (mice or rats) and among themselves they were called *bantu* (one who belongs to their group). They liked drawing meadows where cows pastured. Like the previous group, their families were big cattle raisers. They were forced to leave their herd when attacked by Marshal Mobutu's soldiers. It was said that their culture was based on cattle and milk. They mourned the loss of the herds they had left behind, beyond the border. Many of them were very disheartened by the life they now had to live with neither cattle nor milk. Many of them, it is said, took the road back to Zaire because they could no longer endure life without their herds of cattle. I believe this is why the children in this group liked to draw empty grasslands. Their conversation always centred on cow's milk.

The GP is an acronym for *Garde Presidentielle* (Presidential Guard) and refers to the armed guards of President Juvénal Habyariamana. It is said that these soldiers were the most highly trained in all the army of the Rwandan government at the time. After the death of the President that they were supposed to protect, they began killing the Hutu and Tutsi political opponents and to fight, tooth and nail, against the RPA, these rebels that, rumour had it, had actually killed both President Habyarimana of Rwanda and President Ntaryamira of Burundi. Besides drawing empty caskets, the children in the GP group depicted people, with their arms and legs tied together, being thrown into the rivers. They even named these rivers: the Tanganyika, the Cohoha (Cyohoha), the Akanyaru, and the Ruvubu. This could reflect what they experienced during the events at Ntega and Marangara in Burundi where many killings occurred, as well as in 1993 at the time of the assassination of the Hutu President Melchior Ndadaye. Two children in this group drew crocodiles chomping on human bodies. There were some in this group who described scenes where people were dancing to an orchestra. I couldn't make any sense of this.

The TZ group included the children of former Tutsi refugees from Tanzania, mostly from Kagera and Ngara districts. These children depicted humans being eaten by wild animals such as lions, hyenas, jaguars, and leopards. At the time they entered Rwanda, they probably had to face these wild beasts that were attacking their large livestock. They drew villages burning down. These people were former refugees commonly known as "The refugees of 1959". Most of these refugees owned many assets in Tanzania but unfortunately were forced to leave them behind.

The Sagya was a group of former refugees dating back to 1959. They were the Tutsi from Uganda. They are rarely found in the streets of Kigali and, if by chance, we met one there, they wouldn't reveal anything. They didn't want to talk about the reason that they were living in the streets. Some probably had no parents because they had possibly been killed by the RPA rebels during the war against Rwanda. The big strength of the RPA soldiers was rooted in these former refugees from whom soldiers were recruited. It was, therefore, not surprising that these children became orphans following this war where the RPA lost many soldiers. They made no drawings. They didn't want to. I don't know why.

However, all these children commonly portrayed behaviour expressing intolerance. It was rare that they apologized to anyone or forgave anyone if they had had differences. Also, even if they came from different groups, they did not segregate themselves based on ethnicity. This was a very positive trait. If only the rest of the Rwandan society could only imitate their good example. Instead we officially state that ethnic groups no longer exist, and that information is erased from identification cards, even though we see ongoing prejudice in action in everyday life. Will the divisions that seem to rip apart the same Tutsi groups ever cease? Precedence seems to dictate that the Tutsi from Uganda, like President Paul Kagame, occupy the highest tier. The Tutsi from Tanzania and Kenya occupy the second level. The Tutsi from Burundi, like the First Lady, occupy the third echelon of those in power. Nearly at the bottom of the ladder are the Tutsi from Zaire and the Rwandan survivors. They are reproached due to the fact that they were not victims of the 1994 Genocide, as if they themselves could choose to live or not.

These street kids never learned to relate to others where there is a question of tolerance, forgiveness, and love. Have they not, their whole lives, been subjected to contempt? Have they not learned to distrust each other? How could they not dwell on the atrocities that raised them? They bring out, or represent, the horrors they have been subjected to during their tender childhood years. This horror is externalized whenever the possibility to do so is presented. Bramble bushes only produce bramble bushes. We should worry about what they will become in adulthood!

Of all these children, two of them retained more of my attention. They were too cruel. When they were punished, they would avenge themselves on other children weaker than themselves. When they were prevented from hurting others, they would beat to death any domestic animal at hand. If none were available, they would vent their anger on the shrubs, pulling them out, roots and all. Why this aggressiveness?

Such destructive aggression must absolutely find an object to attack, an outlet. Release is essential for the aggressor, otherwise the pent-up anger eats him up inside—where he is entirely unstable. Have they not, since an early age, learned that there is no relating to others except through aggression and the law of the survival of the fittest? The consequence of missing out on positive relationships from a young age is that they react in the same way that they have seen adults react. This strange behaviour caused me to approach them with more tenderness and affection but also with more attentiveness than I gave to the other children. They demonstrated to me the extent of their capabilities, namely, destruction. Maybe we should not expect too much too soon of them. The names of these children were Mbazende and Ntazina, the real heroes of this testimonial book. Actually, these two boys returned into the streets of Kigali after leaving the Youth Center of Gatenga—this is where I had met them for the first time. It was there that I discovered their bizarre behaviour. It was at Gatenga that they revealed to me what was eating away at their hearts. They had been forced to trek barefoot from Katale to Mbandaka, a long and arduous journey that no known explorer has ever made on horseback or in a vehicle let alone on foot.

It was during this journey into the unknown that they were successively deprived of their father, then their mother. They witnessed many massacres from which they managed to escape. They carry with them the burden of long-endured suffering about which they are not allowed to talk, for fear of being accused of being Genocide perpetrators, negativists, or revisionists. These labels would warrant their death or life imprisonment. Since they bear all this on a daily basis, their subconscious cannot rest. It is impossible. It goes without saying that their spirit is troubled. The traumatizing memory of this tragedy will not allow a harmonious development of their whole being. It's almost impossible to achieve. The behaviour of a child surely reflects what he is feeling inside.

My response to their cruelest and most aggressive behaviour was to show them more love and attention. I even spent entire days with them in the streets of Kigali. I would get home much too late because of the stories they wanted to share with me. They needed more tenderness. As a result, I was allowed to penetrate the walls of their fort, the home into which no one else had been allowed. It was really a Pandora's Box (Cf. Myth of Pandora's Box where opening it unleashed all sorts of evil in the world), but it helped me to understand what motivates their aggressive behaviour. They told me that they would like to have the strength of a lion, even for just a second, to avenge themselves. They were sad about living a dog's life forever. I would tell them a lot of stories to keep them busy and to instruct them too.

Of all the tales I told them, these two children were intrigued by the Bible story of Samson [Judg. 12–13]. The episode they loved to hear me repeat was where he regained his strength and was able to destroy the palace of those who were mocking him. The justification for choosing this one was that Samson was not weak. He died in combat, in avenging himself on his enemies. I understood very well how suffering had marked and wounded these boys. As I spent time with them, I discovered that the overt behaviour of a child depends, sometimes if not always, on what he has lived during his childhood and what he has seen with his own eyes and stored in his subconscious. One cannot always expect too much of them. On the contrary, they need help to better integrate what they have experienced. I made a habit of visiting street kids in the centres that cared for them. There are several types of centres: There are some who take children full-time—like the Youth Centres at Gatenga and Kimisagara—and others that will only keep them occupied during the daytime , like the Red Cross Center in Kacyiru, and send the children back to the streets at night. At Gatenga, every day after morning prayer and the message of the day—a routine for Salesians—I would gather up the children so that they could tell me about the dreams that they had had the night before. For the most part, their dreams consisted of fighting to defend their parents, friends, neighbours, and acquaintances they saw killed. They were defending themselves with the same weapons used by the assassins as Dr. Lawrence E. Shapiro has demonstrated (The secret of Language of Children. How to understand what your kids are really saying? Sourcebooks Inc. Illinois, 2003, pp. 131-137).

One day an 8 year old girl entertained us with her story. She dreamt that she was jumping on the back of a jaguar that was devouring her little brother who had died during the Genocide. In her dream, she had chopped the jaguar into pieces, then ate the meat. It didn't taste good, she said. The girl later caught malaria— a sickness normally transmitted by a female mosquito who injects the protozoa which cause the disease to get into the human bloodstream. When I tried to understand and analyze her dream, I figured out that it fell into the category of symbolic dreams (as inspired by the book of Laurence Benveniste, Le grand dictionnaire des rêves, un voyage initiative au pays des rêves, Goélette editions Longueil, 2005) for it is full of emotion and a depth of feeling that everyday dreams do not evoke. This dream is not logical and the place where it happened is not evident. However, this dream left a powerful impression on the little girl. She was strongly moved by the illusion that she had gained the power to fight and win over the jaguar. As I observed her during the telling of her story, I understood that this was a projection into the future, a way to deal with something that she is not yet strong enough to achieve. This opened a window through which I looked beyond and imagined when this child would be able to make her dream a reality as it is explained by some authors like Ana Freud, Laplanche, etc.[5] I was afraid to examine what was lying beneath this dream, especially when I asked other children about the girl and they told me that *Jaguar* was the nickname of the man who had killed her mother. She had originally come from Kibuye, then directly to Mushubati. According to a typical interpretation of the language of dreams, the jaguar could also represent the destructive force which the world will not resist (Cf. Lauwrence Benveniste, op.cit. article on Jaguar). In the case of these young people, they are undermined by the destructive force of revenge. We have to help them to use that power in a good way, a non-destructive way, by showing them that we love them and that we want to help them.

The Salesians of Don Bosco at Gatenga acknowledge that it was an intriguing experience to work with these children. The Youth Center at Gatenga called *Kwa Carlos* (Chez Carlos) reminded me of the Belgian Red Cross orphanage at Kacyiru where I grew up. In this centre run by the Salesians, children were always busy and received training and formation directed toward the blossoming of the child. Don Carlos, whose nickname was Kiroso because of his long beard that he allowed the children to stroke, surrounded these children with affection. Each child considered him to be his or her father, so much so that every child felt personally very loved and protected. Good Salesian that he was, he considered each child to be unique and each particular problem unique as well. No child resembled any other child and that is why Don Carlos approached every child to listen to him or her, to counsel and to prevent the child from having evil thoughts or acting upon them. At all times, the child was occupied, either playing games, attending morning or evening assemblies, or involved in sports or other healthy pastimes. A Salesian always accompanied the children and, when needed, a trainee would sleep in the dormitory with them. I loved the Salesian

---

5   —It is interesting to read what authors, such as Ana Freud, Laplanche and Pontalis, have to say. It is a defense mechanism called "identification with the aggressor" by either reliving in his own way the aggression as it occurred or by physically or mentally imitating the aggressor or by adopting some powerful symbols that characterize him. Instead of suffering passively, he becomes actively aggressive. This coping mechanism risks making the vulnerable children more virulent and violent in adulthood, a danger to avoid before it is too late.

method of accompanying the children and giving them undivided attention and a feeling of security.

Father Carlos had introduced a sport called acrobatics to Rwanda. It was a type of gymnastics that thrilled spectators, especially the juggling acts and the famous Yoga feats accompanied by good music. I find the Salesian method of education, where the child is constantly involved in sports and hobbies of his or her choice, and always accompanied, to be excellent. The animator, with the help of *Kiroso* (Father Carlos) and the patronage of the children, should get to know and be able to adjust to the temperament of each child. He must succeed in having him or her being accepted in a peer group as well as correcting shortcomings and teaching impulse control. Children can be like clay or marble; they can take on several shapes if they have a good and observant instructor.

I discovered that children themselves are our true teachers because etymologically speaking, is not the pedagogue the one who guides children to the way of the school? We need to imitate their innocence. Father Carlos recognized in me the preferential love that I have for children. I refer to them as my spiritual guides. That is why he brought me along with him whenever he drove the children to different games and acrobatic activities. He didn't hesitate to place in my care any who acted dangerously. The trigger was usually that, without our knowledge, they had taken drugs. Some of these kids in Gatenga had at one time been soldiers in the RPA.

Street Kids In The Refugee Camps Of Zaire

The Mayibobo Street Kids phenomenon was also evident in the camps for displaced persons in the interior of the country as well as in the refugee camps of Zaire and Tanzania We did not really speak of them as street kids because there are no streets in those refugee camps. There, *blindés* (shelters constructed with sheetings and located side by side) did not allow the establishment of streets. This is why they were called "ENA" (Enfants Non-Accompagnés/ Unaccompanied children). To survive, they had to organize themselves into groups of two or three and scour the countryside, begging for food because the rations served by the WFP (World Food Programs) were not ample. They would steal objects from their neighbours, especially sheetings and clothing that they resold for food or take on work that was beyond their strength. They could, for example, go into the forest near the Katale camp and gather up firewood, a task even the adults could not accomplish. A degree of unprecedented promiscuity was prevalent so the girls could sacrifice themselves to prostitution. In certain refugee camps, there were real brothels like "Moto Moto's" in Mugunga and "Mbogo's" in Katale, etc.

Firstly, the systematic destruction of the family, followed by the elimination of the moral personality and models of the children and finally the massacres at the camps where innumerable people lost their lives, all contributed to the demise of the orphans. They were left to fend for themselves, either by retracing their steps to repatriate, by joining the increasing ranks of street kids or by wandering in the forests of Zaire, fleeing the killings and massacres designed to wipe all Rwandan and Burundian refugees from the face of the earth. Several common graves were found in the former refugee camps or surrounding area. Refugees would have been killed at any point along their journey. It is during this unknown—or perhaps voluntarily ignored—massacre that more than half of those living in the camps disappeared.

ANTIPODEAN RWANDAN SOCIETY
MAYIBOBO, A REFLECTION OF THE DECLINING RWANDAN SOCIETY

Do we need to speak of the "Mayibobo" phenomenon as the sour grapes of Rwandan society? How do we explain the social exclusion of these street kids, if not in terms of psychosis in which the mentally-ill are unaware of its existence?

Over and over again, they tell us that Rwanda is regenerating itself. Is it emerging from its ashes? We hope so, because a beautiful flower can only grow where a seed, that has already died, finds itself reinvigorated; in this miraculous way, life is brought forth from death. Who can germinate life from the Genocide against the Tutsi and the deadly massacre by the Hutu?

"The blood of the martyrs is the seed of Christianity," says Tertullian, the first of the Christians to write in Latin. What becomes of the blood shed by Rwandans? I leave this question to the Rwandans themselves and to those who are helping them in their mutual destruction. What have we gained by killing each other? What I am certain of is that we have left a legacy of widows, orphans, and Mayibobo to our country. We must offer to these children, orphans, and Mayibobo—to these seeds that are already dead, and whose lives are in slow motion or in dormancy—new lives. They must be afforded an adequate environment on the affective, materialistic, physical and educational levels, in surroundings that guarantee safety for all. In short, they must be given the opportunity to blossom into beautiful flowers.

I believe—and with good reason—that every child, whether born of a Tutsi, a Hutu, or a Twa—whether aware of it or not—needs a basic education. A child has a right to an education, to wholesome and nutritional food, to shelter and access to basic health services. He needs to be treated like every other child that he sees around him, without being told that he is genocidal. It is at this price, and only at this price, of not categorizing children as good or bad, of not deeming them animals to knock down because of what their parents did that we could hope for life sprouting up from the humus of Rwandan society. What quality of life is owed to Rwandans? Everyone must ask themselves this fundamental question.

The phenomenon of which we are speaking constitutes a problem that preoccupies all those concerned with the reconstruction of our society. But reconstructing the country does not refer only to the basic infrastructure and the up-to-date technology that is the vision of our country—see the policy of the Vision for 2010! It must also include the moral reconstruction, which implies the development of man in all his dimensions.

I am referring to persons whose development in the inter-personal dimension is arrested—an issue that should concern all people. It refers equally to persons stuck in their relations with others living in the same society. This development must, therefore, concern each and every person as members of this society as a whole. A person, to be fully human, should be educated, thus humanizing base, animalistic tendencies. Blaise Pascal has said it well: "Man is neither an angel nor a beast; he who wants to be an angel acts like a beast."

The country has an obligation to facilitate the physical, psychological re-adaptation as well as the social reintegration of these children who were abandoned and left on their own, the victims of human wickedness. This should take place under conditions that favour good health, self-respect as well as respect for the human race. Otherwise, who knows whether these same children will one day, like a rattlesnake coming out of its hiding place to strike with venom, become avengers of the social injustices to which they have been subjected. If this problem is not addressed, our country will become a battlefield for infernal wars and visceral hatred even more deadly than the Genocide. Any poison that is swallowed, unless immediately regurgitated, will kill the person who swallowed it. Who, even if he or she had strong antibodies, could live for a long time with an open wound not tended to? This is our Rwandan society, a sick person not being taken care of, a country seated atop Nyiragongo, a volcano that sooner or later will erupt.

THEIR DEEPEST WOUNDS

With the help of analytical, normative, and descriptive approaches, targeting respectively the causes, the norms, and the values they developed as well as the conditions of their lamentable lives, I will attempt to show that these children are living with wounds that are deep and infected—wounds that influence all aspects of their being. They do not like to expose them, thereby contributing enormously to the ongoing neglect. These wounds are ingrained on the physical, emotional, and intellectual levels.

Harmony of the Three Dimensions of the Human Person[6]

Like all people, the Mayibobo street kids need to build character in all three human dimensions: the sensory (physical), emotional (feelings) and the spiritual (intellectual).

Sensory Level

The sensory level (physical) constitutes all that is bodily, including physical strength. Here we must remember that a living person is not just an assembly of muscles attached to bones by tendons and ligaments as well as a collection of organs connected by blood vessels and nerve bundles in an abdominal cavity! A living person is more than that. He or she is a living organism, which means that all the components—cells, tissue, organ and systems—are in perfect harmony to the extent that, if one part suffers, all others suffer as well. It should be like this for the Rwandan society. Just as each component of the human body works for the well-being of the others, each member of this body, namely the Rwandan society, should be concerned with the physical, mental, and intellectual well-being of the other members of the same society.

A person is composed not only of a body, but also of a living soul and a living spirit. To look at him or her otherwise is to diminish the person, to reduce him or her to a body, or a powerful robot. Many street kids exhibit problems at this basic level. Over a long period of time, they endured fatigue, hunger, and a long journey whose destination was unknown and are now doing work that surpasses their capacity as children. What are they eating today? They ferret out discarded foods from the garbage cans. They drug themselves to forget their misery and to sleep worry-free. If they become what they eat, who will stop them? As they themselves say: *"Twariye umwanda"* (We have eaten the inedible), which means that they are

---

6   My analysis is inspired by: Joyce Meyer. Battlefield Of The Mind, Winning The Battle In Your Mind, New York 2011; Michel Quoist. Construire l'homme 1997 ; Pascale Ide. Construire sa personnalité, Serment/Fayard 1997 ; Pascale Ide. Connaître ses blessures, Editions de l'Emmanuel Fayard 1999 ; Pascal Ide. Mieux se connaître pour mieux s'aimer, Editions du Jubilé/ Fayard, 1998 ; Pascal Ide. Les neufs portes de l'âme, l'ennéagramme, Editions du Jubilé, 1999

ready to do anything regardless of the cost. They are the rejects of society just as we speak of graft rejection in Biology. They live with a deep-seated inferiority complex—so much so that they feel less than human—since they compare themselves to other children who are living a normal life with their parents. This provokes in them psychological suffering, timidity, anguish, fear, hostility, aggressiveness, and a need to surpass others and to boss them around. This attitude is a natural reaction and a subconscious one. It controls their every action. Our street kids are suffering; they are seeking—at the very least—peace of mind and employing any means that they can to get it.

They will resort to any method that serves the defence mechanism of their crippled identities. Although they are suffering, they are seeking a solution to their lifestyle by taking drugs to dull the pain, the fear, the shyness, the feelings of inferiority, etc. It is because of these drugs that the children have no fear. Physically, they rely on sleeping pills and tranquilizers like gasoline, glue, and hemp, etc. Psychologically, they will seek to oppose power when they feel powerless, dominance when they are being dominated, and aggressiveness in the face of feelings of incompetence, intolerance and incomprehension, all by reason of compensation. We are in the process of grooming tyrants, dominators, authoritarians, dictators, intolerants, and cynics—people who will not give up and who feel no pity. They will act like people who obey only street law— or more accurately, *jungle* law! It is the street, its logic, and what it represents as a framework for life that has formed them. This is the heritage that we have reserved for our future society. Herein lies the realization of the Rwandan "Vision 2020" (Cf. Http://www.minecofin. gov.rw/webfml). Based on the premise of a hierarchy of needs, since their physical needs are left unsatisfied, it follows that these children are also suffering emotionally and manifesting it psychologically. If they are physically exhausted, they are unable to open up in their relationships with others and psychologically, they are depressed.

Affective Level

The affective dimension (heart) is the seat of feelings of tolerance, affection, and love. Here again, one must remember that a living person is not made of sentiment alone. We know people who are too sentimental, a trait that can be abundantly harmful to others. Even if, as Blaise Pascal suggests, "the heart has reasons of which reason is not aware," the heart needs the physical body and a living spirit to be a harmoniously balanced person. The role of the mind is to co-ordinate and to command the actions of a living and normal human being. The body will act upon what it senses the mind is telling it to do. This is the only way that the will would be able to follow through with the desire. Our children are injured at the affective level. We have to think about how to dress the festering wounds suffered as a result of lack of affection. Yes, these children, rejected by society, consider themselves to be cursed by God, hated not just in their world but by the entire world as well. If they grow up to be tyrants or terrorists, as we know is possible based on past history in the world, we should not be surprised. We will reap what we have sown.

Their hearts are broken, a fact which will not leave our society unscathed. Whoever wishes for a better society, and one that will last for a long time, must start to show tenderness to these children whose hearts have been shattered. We must definitely approach them. These children have endured so much that it has made them cold as ice and hard as nails. If they are left with open wounds, they will without a doubt repay society for the injustices inflicted upon them because, as is often said, "What goes around comes around!" Thus, everything that they are storing in their subconscious, like an atomic bomb on Nagasaki or Hiroshima, will explode on us. If the family would take up its role of home where love radiates, it could repair the affective dimension of these children.

SPIRITUAL LEVEL

The spiritual level (the intellect) is the domain of all that is cognitive, of liberty, free will, and intelligence. A person who acts only upon what reason dictates, without taking into consideration his heart—love, compassion, mercy, goodness, forgiveness etc.—would be no different than a computer. Before a good decision can be made, humans must think of others and how they would be affected as a consequence of said decision. This would be acting responsibly. Tyrants are people who act selfishly, without taking into account the hurtful effect on society. The spiritual dimension is impacted in an important way in children who are of age but do not attend school. Our children are at risk of being perpetually illiterate because of a lack of personnel and necessary educational supplies.

I myself witnessed an upsetting situation: a widow from Bugesera in Gashora municipality was hitting her daughter who had just told her mother that she had passed the high school entrance exam. Her mother hurled insults at her and beat her with a stick. She behaved in this way, not because passing the exam was an embarrassment to the family—on the contrary if we consider how few went to secondary school—but because she was frustrated, for she was unable to pay the tuition—the lesser of two evils would have been that her daughter fail the exam. At least, then, this mother would have had peace of mind and the child would have suffered less. Similar cases are found in all the villages of Rwanda. If this young girl had not received assistance from neighbours in the parish where I was, she would probably have ended up in the streets, exposed to prostitution like the other Mayibobo girls. In what society will uneducated children live, if ours aspires only to becoming more technological? Their learning environments are the markets, the roadways, gas stations, pubs, stadiums, crossroads, large neighbourhoods, bridges, and the floorboards of vehicles. What calibre of man or woman could possibly emerge from these dirty classrooms? Let's wait and see. Don't forget that we can only reap what we have sown. The education refused to them will be compensated for in one way or another. The development of these outcasts of society is unbalanced. They eat poorly or not at all and strap themselves to work beyond their physical capacity. In compensation, they take drugs and tranquilizers. These are our adults of tomorrow. They are destructive forces in the making. All of society has been warned. All of humanity should respond this time.

Since man is a social creature, the street kid who does not find an adequate framework in which to develop socially, will construct one for himself. It will be a society in which he moves freely, without control or social constraint. In the end, he will push away anyone who is not like him. If a street kid is not adequately formed at these three levels, he will alienate himself from society. He could be seen as a stumbling block for this society that is evolving without him. We could then conclude with this Latin adage: *"sub mele latet veninum"* (Under the honey lies the venom)—under the honey, which is the development of some rich Kigali neighbourhoods, lies the venomous dissatisfaction of a starving population of Mayibobo, wallowing in misery. In 2006, more than 60% of Rwandans were living below the level of poverty and 50% of this population did not have what they needed to live (https://www.cia.gov/library/publications/the-world-factbook/geos/rw.html). What would happen tomorrow if the good of society were reclaimed by this blacklisted society?

THE FAMILY, TRIPARTITE IN NATURE OR NON-EXISTENT

A family is generally and ideally composed of a father, a mother, and children. We could compare this to the traditional Rwandan *iziko* (cooking fire source or home) in which the hearth is composed of hearthstones—three rocks placed in the shape of a triangle. If one of these rocks fails to hold, the pot or frying pan falls. If one of these three elements in our traditional home is missing, *"rimwe rirabura bakaburara"* (we go to bed with an empty stomach). The father would be like the hearthstone on the right, the mother, the one on the left and the child would be the one in the back. Keep in mind that a triangle has dimensions, an area, a base and a height. For myself, I consider the equilateral triangle, where all sides are equal, to be the best one. It would be an ideal model for the perfect family where the qualities of each are shared with the other two. These two hearthstones do all they can to keep the child in the back in balance. It is only on condition that the three are solid, that we could successfully place the pot on top without it spilling over. The cooking fire is the love between the couple, which only makes sense when it is reciprocal. The husband lives for the love of his wife and vice versa. To blossom, the child needs the continuous love of both parents. For an orphan child or one who has lost one parent, a grave imbalance occurs. A great number of children have lost one of their parents, or both of them at the same time. Many have helplessly witnessed the murder of their parents, brothers, uncles, aunts, cousins, godfathers, and godmothers. For most of them, the extended family has been decimated or annihilated. This constitutes a big handicap to the balanced development of these children.

Usually, in the course of development, the child demonstrates a preference in showing affection toward others based on age and sex. For example, the little boy who loves his mother wants her all to himself and is jealous of his father. The little girl, who loves her dad, wants him all to herself and is jealous of the mother. It is definitely necessary for a child to go through this stage to ensure a healthy emotional, relational, and sexual development. Evidently, we must keep in mind that, if this tendency persists beyond adolescence, it is considered to be abnormal. A boy would become more feminine if he identified more with his mother and became fixated on her. It would be impossible for him, then, to be well-balanced. A girl, who identifies more so with her father and becomes fixated on him, would become more masculine. It would also be impossible for her to be able to really love affectionately even if she were to marry. On the other hand, the father is perceived, through the eyes of the child, to be a symbol of strength and glory. For the child, the father has superhuman characteristics and is placed on a pedestal above all other living beings. He represents strength, glory, infallibility and is the symbol of radiance. A child who loses his or her father at a young age is deprived of this model, and a balanced development is at risk. In the loss of the father, the child also loses the sense of *pater genitor* (father who gives life), *pater familiae* (father who takes care of the family), and *pater protector* (powerful father who assures the security and protection of the family). These children have not only lost their parents, but more importantly, their powerlessness and nakedness—literally for some of them—has been exposed. When all is said and done, all human beings are fragile in this way. In the eyes of a child, no one is more powerful than their parents, especially the father. If the parents are shown to be powerless, then all men are considered powerless. In whom can they then believe and trust? In men, who have proven to be powerless? Should they believe in some greater power such as God who proved to be powerless by not protecting the child's loved ones. Does an intermediary exist? Not at all! It's understandable that their integration is difficult.

If we consider an analogy of a scale where three trays are equally balanced, the family depends on these three trays—father, mother, children—being simultaneously in balance so it can thrive. Authors like Cloutier state precisely that the harmonious development of the child correlates with the sensitivity of the parent toward the child and the clarity of messages given to him or her. These children certainly do not live in a society that is sensitive to their needs. The message that society is trying to transmit to them clashes with the child's incomprehension of the insane, adult world and the insensitivity and lack of concern of this society striving to grow and develop without them. Society must present itself as compassionate and comprehensive, and above all, must adapt to this new lifestyle. Over and above that, it must uproot all existing seeds of war and death. Let's go back to the trays on the scale; if one tray is off-balance, it will assuredly affect the other two. Imagine then, what the situation would be if the scale has only two trays in balance. Here, the child who felt so secure in the heart of a well-balanced family where the parents assure him all is well, abruptly loses his parents. He becomes traumatized and the scale depolarizes. When this child still has a little brother, he loses his bearings in this new situation. His instincts would tell him that he must, ipso facto, replace his parents in caring for his little brother.

If it is true that the blind cannot lead the blind, it also holds true that one child cannot properly educate another. It adds to the disequilibrium. This is a gaping, open wound in his life. Unless the child finds a surrogate family who would provide the role of father and mother, one where the child could blossom and identify with the parent according to gender and age, he or she cannot mature effectively. It would be impossible for such a child to become a truly loving being. How would one get a sense that the world is good? There are eloquent legends and myths that address this subject, such as the child raised by a female wolf who bore some characteristics of wolf behaviour. One raised by a lion becomes like a lion. Now what would we expect a child, who had nothing but bandits, prostitutes and other Mayibobo as models, to resemble? These children suffer from an unlovable complex and strong feelings of culpability. These children think that they are even cursed by God himself. They feel rejected by all humanity. They feel that they have no right to live a life like other children. They like to think of themselves as already dead. They, therefore, have no fear of dying again. When one is sad, the world is black and inspires disgust and hostility.

"A Dead Goat No Longer Fears The Knife"

Children such as these always carry a knife in their pocket, ready to react defensively against anyone who attacks. It is the survival instinct, pushed to extreme limits, that motivates such behaviour. They are educated in violence because the world they inhabit is a world of violence. Living surrounded daily by violence assures that they will become violent. This is how a wise Rwandan proverb explains this premise: *"Ihene mbi ntawe uyizirikaho iye"* (One cannot tether together a bad goat with a good goat lest the one who was good, become corrupted).

Violence only gives rise to a vicious circle of more violence. For these children, the world is menacing. Humanity acts inhumanely, and so one must protect oneself. Such a child acts without fear since he considers himself already dead. He also considers those around him to be dead like him, and therefore he thinks nothing of sending them to their grave!

To counteract this model of violence, we need to establish a model of love because love grows by loving and gives rise to only more love. Love is like a good perfume; its fragrance permeates and can spread far. When love is shown, it transforms immensely the one being loved, for those being shown love see themselves as lovable beings. It expands to many visions and to the universe. Only love can build up humanity, a humanity these children were unable to find in the world around them. The same instinct of self-preservation and protection is seen in action when, for example, someone comes to help settle differences between two Mayibobo who are arguing—with one common agenda, the two of them together attack the outsider and beat him to death if he is not strong enough to fend them off.

In Kigali one day, we witnessed such a scene. While two Mayibobo were brawling, a police officer intervened. He soon found himself being attacked by both of them. At the same time, many other Mayibobo flew to the aid of their comrades. They managed to take his gun. They yelled at him, "Put your hands up or we'll shoot!" This officer would have gotten a bullet to the head had not another police officer interrupted by jumping on the child poised to open fire. There ensued a tough battle between the Mayibobo and Police who were hit by stones. These children aren't afraid of anything. What surprised me even more was that, while this scuffle was going on, the other children were attacking anything at all. The first targets were evidently all luxury items such as cars and motorcycles.

One would have thought that they were all suffering from claustrophobia. This behaviour is justified by Martin Luther King's statement: "An injustice committed anywhere is a threat to justice in the entire world." A society of individuals who fear nothing and who obey only the laws of the jungle will breed more individuals like themselves. Our society is reaping the hatred that it has sown. Today's humiliated and frustrated child will become tomorrow's neurotic adult. To compensate, he will search for power and domination, which will shape him or her to be a dictator, a cynic, and a tyrant. History has taught us much about the direction this can take. Here is a story that took place in Nyarutarama, a new neighbourhood in Kigali designed for the rich:

A young lad who had to guide his blind grandfather with the help of a stick, threw a stone that hit a grey car, a Mercedes-Benz Jeep. What came of it?

You see, the boy's grandfather had fallen ill and needed to be transported by car to the dispensary. His grandson went out to the road to hail down a passing vehicle, but no one stopped. The young man was so discouraged that he began throwing stones at every vehicle that passed by.

This is how he happened to break the rear-view mirror of the grey Benz Jeep. The driver, an important businessman with a big belly, stopped the Jeep, chased the rascal, caught him, and began lashing out at him. After hitting him, he grabbed him, "Come on, peasant boy, I'm driving you to the police station in Remera."

"Before you do that," the boy pleaded, "will you help me to take my grandfather, who is seriously ill, to the sos dispensary down there? Then you can take me wherever you want, for I am not afraid to die."

Our important gentlemen was moved. His heart tormented him so strongly that he agreed to help. He accepted the invitation to come into the house where he found the blind grandfather in agony. The old man scolded his grandson for not yet having taken him to the hospital. The boy explained that none of the neighbours wanted to help them and that no vehicles had wanted to stop. That was why he had decided to throw stones at every vehicle that passed by him. Not only did the rich fellow drive the blind man to Roy Fayçal Hospital (one of the most expensive in Kigali) but he paid all his hospital costs and decided to adopt the boy after the grandfather passed away.

We need to congratulate all these people who give of themselves for the cause of abandoned children in need. In helping them, one not only contributes to their survival but also rebuilds their confidence in other human beings because, so often, the situation in which they are living is the result of human cruelty.

By acting accordingly, they are also aiding society. One never knows. The child you save along the way may someday become someone great. Einstein was a refugee! Furthermore, it is said that Adolf Hitler's development was thwarted in adolescence! A child is like a block of marble from which many statues could potentially be carved. He is like clay that could be modelled into many shapes. From it could emerge a genius who could save the entire society or a malefactor who could put this society into ruin. *"Utazi agakura yima umwana."* (He who knows not the potential, refuses to give the child what he asks).

EPILOGUE

Why have I decided to review this book and to update it? I felt that the original, RWANDA, L'HUMAIN TROP INHUMAIN (Humanity Too Inhumane) was quickly written and contained many careless errors and a lack of precision. In this book, I hope to correct those errors and to adapt the content. Also, certain chapters have been revised and reordered.

In revising this book, I have tried to satisfy the requests of a good number of people who have expressed to me what they would like to see as content in a testimonial book of this calibre. Notwithstanding, I have knowingly made no mention of appeals from extremists on all sides who have accused me of leaning too heavily on the side of the Hutu, for example, in my stories. Many of my Tutsi friends have reproached me for not being ashamed by exposing the suffering of the Hutu population in Zaire while they were being sought by the Tutsi extremists in power in Kigali. Moreover, some of them had the audacity to accuse me of not conferring with them in the preparation of this present book. Nevertheless, every person who approached me about these matters never stepped one foot in Zaire at the time that the Hutu refugee camps were being destroyed by the Government of Kigali who had decided to kill this majority population, quasi-innocent of the Genocide of the Tutsi.

Also, soon after I had published my book about the massacres of the refugees in the camps of Zaire, a report from the ONU[7] concerning the so-called massacres was published. It contained many interesting details about these massacres, meticulously organized and inhumanely executed, as well as the destruction of Hutu refugee camps in Zaire. The report also accuses the RPA of having organized and carried out these massacres. The report even dares to classify these massacres as Genocide, something I would not have dared to

---

7   Report on the Mapping Project concerning the most serious violations against human rights and international humanitarian rights committed between March 1993 and June 1993 in the Democratic Republic of the Congo, 2010 Report

do. I am still being accused of not having addressed the Genocide of the Tutsi in my book. In fact, being constrained by the delimitation of the subject and considering, moreover, that there already exists a plethora of literature on the subject, I thought it wise to not alter the testimony of these two children who were former Hutu refugees in the camps of Zaire.

On the other hand, my second book *Rwanda, Pays Où La Mort Règne En Maître Absolu* (Rwanda, Where Death Rules as Absolute Master) does address the Genocide of the Tutsi. It deals with the rejection of the Tutsis, the same Tutsis who in the past were victims of the hatred of Hutu extremists, victims of those who pretended to take up arms to defend them. I published both these books simultaneously because, in my mind, they complemented each other in informing anyone interested in knowing the sufferings of the Rwandan people as it is mentioned in that report. A third book, completing the series of testimonies, will also be published shortly.

I have not only been attacked by the Tutsi extremists, who without shame or hesitation have classified me as an Interahamwe. They said this, not on the basis that I might have killed any Tutsis, but because I have dared to tell what happened to Hutu people in Zaire. I dared to break the interdict of the Rwandan Government who kills everyone who has tried to open his mouth about these murders in Zaire. Curiously, President Kagame himself and the Generals Faustin Kayumba Nyamwasa and James Kabarebe who led this killing in Zaire admitted to having perpetrated these atrocities. One must listen to the speech given by President Kagame Paul, in which he states that he regrets not having been able to exterminate all the Hutu who were in Rwanda in 1994 or those who were in Zaire in 1996 (Cf. The speech of President Kagame Paul in Murambi on April 7, 2007). All of these friends who called me an Interahamwe know full well what the designation of Interahamwe implies and the penalty it could incur, even upon people who are in exile or in western countries: The Rwandan government doesn't hesitate to send assassins into these countries to murder those who dare to divulge the ugly secrets of the government, what it doesn't want the world to know. Nevertheless, I don't bear any grudge against them if they, too, are not motivated by a visceral hatred that would automatically make anyone denounce the misdeeds of the Kigali government. They feel sorry for me, labelling me a negativist, who dares to speak up about something that the Kigali Government wants kept silent. They would burn these truths and then scatter the ashes into the forests and streams just as they did with the corpses of the Hutu refugees that they ordered killed in the camps and forests of Zaire.

What convinced me that there are some Rwandans who are sick of ethnicity is the accusation coming from the Hutu extremist milieu. They are accusing me of being too lenient toward the Tutsi because I only relayed the testimony of two children instead of speaking openly of all that I saw with my own eyes as a survivor of Tutsi vengeance against the Hutu refugees in Zaire, where hundreds of thousands were murdered by the RPA.

The fact is that I could not intersperse my testimony with that of these two innocent children who never had any idea of what was going on in Rwanda. Nor did I want to include, in one book, the testimonies of many survivors of the Genocide, firstly because there is already a plethora of literature in this domain, and secondly, because each situation was totally different. The testimonies of those who were, in the first instance, victims of the wicked Hutu, then victims of the Tutsi, will be included in my next two books.

As for myself, who grew up in Rwanda and was subjected to this Rwandan evil since 1990, the peak of which was in 1994, I have given my own testimony. There is much commonality between what I have seen, lived, suffered, and what others have repeated to me about their experiences. It is true that the Genocide took many of my relatives and some of my close friends. I myself survived the massacres perpetrated on the soil of both Rwanda and Zaire. Each time that I reminisce on my life, I recognize that God was always at my side to protect me from danger. In my upcoming, autobiographical book soon to be published, I will speak in the first person about what I have seen.

Finally, as a Rwandan priest, I would like to respond to a question that is frequently asked of me: "Why are you alive, whereas the others of your generation, or many of those who were with you, are dead?"

My reflection on this subject will be very short. Once and for all, I could say that I am still alive, despite having been the object of innumerable solicitations by Death, because the Lord had a mission in mind for me. What mission? You and I are both awaiting the details. I am convinced of this mission, and at the end of the day, I don't worry about what tomorrow will bring. I've had a lot of opportunities to die, but God has spared my life. Therefore, I cannot let myself be intimidated by anything because maybe my mission is to die at the hands of my brother—Hutu or Tutsi, it doesn't matter—who is not happy to be reminded of what he did or neglected to do in order to save his brother.

There are some Rwandan brothers who are afraid to hear the naked truth. Since I have come to realize to what extent Rwandan wickedness has achieved a level of paroxysm, I have decided to also publish a poetry collection. In these fables, animals speak of people in general and of Rwandans in particular, just as they have found them. Rwandans decide to kill other Rwandans, even though they are not motivated by this instinct to seek nourishment in the manner of these wild, carnivorous animals which do kill for food. But, there again, one must take note of this difference: these wild animals never kill or feed upon those of their family or class. The Rwandan, on the other hand, is moved to kill his own brother, with whom he shares the same blood (Rwandan), the same country (Rwanda), the same culture (Rwandan), the same faith (in Imana, the only God, creator of everything) and above all, the same language (Kinyarwanda)! Is there not, inherent in this, an inhumane wickedness for which the animals have a right to reproach us?

CONCLUSION
PEACE OF HEART IS TRULY
THE HEART OF PEACE[8]

Based on the knowledge of the absurd past, what must follow? Another absurdity? We could be deaf to the lessons that history teaches. What good is history, if not to shed light on the present and to put us on guard for the future? Otherwise, life would be an endless reversion and history an eternal beginning again. I believe this to be false. We must ensure that history does not repeat itself. Since every history is a political history, all political reflection should be based on what really did happen, which presupposes an objective analysis of this history. Hence, history would be like a trampoline launching us into a future full of hope, a future where life is good.

There are three things that I dream will happen before I die and the fourth would give me sweet repose. That Rwanda, once again, become *"Ce Paradis peuplé par la paix"* (A paradise of peaceful people) as it used to be known, one that our poets and musicians aspire to in their songs. I dream that the country might, once again, become the "Cradle" where brothers live peacefully side by side and leaders are concerned for the good of the people. A country for everyone, even for the low class society, Batwa, who today are being squelched. I dream of a country where everyone enjoys freedom of speech without fearing the *"Hematologists"* (those who enjoy shedding the blood of their brothers). I dream of a Rwanda where it's wonderful to live without fear of being suppressed or put to death. How overjoyed I would be on the day that I would hear that all Rwandans eat twice a day and until their hunger is satisfied. This bothers me a great deal. I would be very happy to know that God still spends the night in my dear country as He has in the past. God spent the days elsewhere but He spent the nights in Rwanda *"Imana*

---

8   I was guided in my comments by Most reverend Bishop Fulton J. Sheen Fulton J.Sheen, Peace of soul, Whittlesey House, New York and Toronto, 1949

yirirwa ahandi igataha i Rwanda" as we say and not without reason. We are not sure if He still spends all night in this country or indeed if He even dares put His foot there, if even for a second!

Rwanda today is home to a population who, in a sense, still walks with arms and legs bound together behind their backs as if they were being tortured by the famous Akandoyi. There are those whose eyes are knowingly blindfolded—or voluntarily closed—so that they will not see what is going on. If by chance they should happen to open their eyes, they would have to shut their mouths to avoid being beheaded so that the eyes (that have seen something), the ears (that have heard something) and the mouth (that can attest to something) are gone for good. Therein lies the cavern that the philosopher Plato did not address, because here, even the one-eyed person is not authorized to live for a long time. He is eliminated or forced to live in exile. He may be lucky enough to get a visa or to escape prison alive where half of his life would be devoted to *TIG* (Public Works) which is nothing other than forced labour. As far as visas, many paid a fortune to get one and many girls and beautiful ladies were granted one in exchange for sexual favours. But woe to those who did obtain a visa under those conditions, only to be prevented by the Directorate of Military Intelligence (DMI) from boarding the plane at Kanombe. What a story! What a life! In any case, live and learn!

I think that it is not too pretentious or daring to apply the "Myth of Sisyphus" to what the Burundians, the Congolese, and the Rwandans have endured in the last decade. We have been confronted with much violence, many killings, and barbaric acts that have cast gloom over our respective countries.

According to this myth, Sisyphus could have tricked Death. Actually when Death sought to trap him and take him away, Sisyphus chained Death up and ran away. It was only after quite some time that Zeus, the supreme god, realizing that people were no longer dying, sent Ares, the god of War, Destruction, and Carnage to free Death. Sisyphus, realist that he was, remembered that all men had to die someday as expressed in the wise adage *"Quis quis es morrieris"* (No matter who you are, you will, one day, die). According to his plan, he ordered his wife not to make any funeral arrangements or to mourn him when he died. Following his death, he descended to the underworld and when he met Hades, the god of death, asked permission to return to the living to demand a funeral service. Once he returned to the world of the living, he refused to go back to the world of the dead. Hermes, messenger of the Gods, was forced to chain up Sisyphus and bring him back to the world of the dead. The name of Sisyphus could be given to the Burundian people. The analogy is appropriate because of what the race had to suffer and endure, a race solicited by Death since 1972 during the "unprecedented massacres" and in 1988 during the events at Ntega and Marangara. Recently, in Burundi, there were a series of silent killings, following the assassination of President Melchior Ndadaye in October of 1993. Six months later another Burundian President, Cyprian Ntaryamira was killed along with the Rwandan President, Juvénal Habyarimana on April 6th 1994. All of these assassinations were followed by large scale massacres.

Death had taken on a human face and was embodied in the extremists on both sides, Hutu and Tutsi. Luckily, there were humans—the Hutu and Tutsi non-extremists—who were able to resist Death and chained him up for a while just as Sisyphus did. The Zairians themselves, were to suddenly be butting heads with Death who was on tour in the Great Lakes Region. In the east, Zaire had to measure its strength against Death who had just spent time in Rwanda where he took on a body, a name, and a task unique to him: unspeakable massacres. Since October 1996, this race of people has had to resist him. Even if several million people, the spoils of Death from Uvira to Mbandaka and Kinshasa, succumbed, the Zairians were still able to chain up Death. Otherwise, he had sworn to seize everyone he met. With the assassination of the Rwandan President Juvénal Habyarimana began a cycle of violence and only God knew when it would end. For 100 days, the duration of the Genocide, the Rwandan "survivors" had to hold their head up high in the face of Death personified. Other Rwandans had been butting heads with Death for four years. Death had threatened a hecatomb in Rwanda whose kingdom has given birth to killers from both sides (Hutu and Tutsi). Death had activated all of its lethal mechanisms[9].

The killing methods used by both sides are detailed in the book by Lieutenant Abdul Joshua Ruzibiza, Rwanda, l'Histoire Secrète (Rwanda's Secret Story), Panama Edition, 2005. I am merely repeating them here.

On the part of the Interahamwe:
- Using a machete, splitting a person in half from head to toe if possible;
- Using a studded cudgel to shatter the head with one blow;
- Using grenades to eliminate masses;
- Babies and little children were thrown against walls and died, crushed from the impact;
- Girls were sometimes killed after being raped;
- Fœtus were taken out.

The Inkotanyi used similar techniques or some that they devised themselves:
- They would tie the legs one at a time behind the back and pull until the chest exploded. While they were tied up like this, the person would be stabbed several times;
- Tie up the victims, put a plastic bag over their head and leave them to die of suffocation;
- Tie up the person and with a syringe then fill the ear canal with gasoline. Death would ensue;
- Tie a cord around the neck. Make the person lie on the ground and tighten the rope until death occurred;
- Tightly tie the victim's arms and legs and hang them upside down on the gallows;
- Cutting the victim little by little and burning the skin with pieces of searing hot plastic, as well as pricking sexual parts with needles, especially males in their testicles;

---

9   Read the testimonies of survivors from the two camps as well as the eloquent statements of ex-soldiers of the RPA, especially that of Ruzibiza Abdul (Http://www.rwanda-info.net/index.php).

- Kill girls and women, after having sexually abused
  them, sometimes violently mutilating their bodies. It was not uncommon that they had posts
  or tree trunks rammed into their genitalia;
- The children and babies were hurled head first
  against walls. They died of crushed skulls.

Other testimonies affirm that very often the Inkotanyi forced
mothers to grind their babies with a huge mortar and pestle. They
even forced them to eat their baby's flesh, crushed in these mortars,
to avoid being atrociously killed. Such blind obedience was rewarded
by an easy death which meant a blow to the head with an *Igihozo*
(worn-down hoe). This killed the victim instantly which was prefer-
able to facing torture and mutilation in front of their families. These
mothers suffered great emotional torment, as well, in being forced
to assist powerlessly in the killing or abusing of their own children.

Death had come to Rwanda from the north-east and had taken
up residence since October 1990. Numerous were the soldiers of
Death and many were his victims. Others escaped his traps and
have fettered him for some time. That is what prevented him from
taking all Rwandans, even though he had vowed to make them all
his prey. Among his victims were Tutsis, whose lot had been cast by
the Hutu extremists. Equally, there were Hutus who escaped Death
during the massacres, perpetrated by the Tutsi extremists such as the
RPA. Also, many Twas were seized by Death in their area during the
massacres by the Hutu and Tutsi extremists. They were victimized
by two extremist factions. Unfortunately, no one ever talks about
their murders.

Anyone from these two groups of killers, who escaped Death
personified, is considered to have chained up Death whose goal was
to seize everyone encountered on Rwandan soil. This also included
strangers who did not uphold the view and tactics of the extremists.
Yes, I include strangers because during this period of time, there
were soldiers, UN Peacekeepers (MINUAR) under the direction of
Canadian General Romeo Dalaire. Some of his troops lost their lives
in this country. The Belgians, "Les Dix Casques Bleus Belges" (The

Ten Belgian Blue Helmets) were killed in Rwanda by the Ex-RAF. Also, there were many ex-patriots who were assassinated during this period of time, among other Spanish and Canadian priests. For example: the Canadian priest, Fr. Claude Simard, assassinated in his parish at Ruyenzi on October 17th. 1994; Canadian Fr. Guy Pinard assassinated while celebrating Mass in his parish in Kampanga on February 2nd. 1997; Spanish Fr. Joachim Vallmajo Sala killed on April 26th. 1994 at Byumba; Spanish Fr. Isidro Uzcundun Pouso killed at Mugina on January 10th. 2000; Fr. Croite Vjecko killed on January 31st. 1998 in Kigali; Spanish Fr. Sevando Mayor Garcia, Brother Miguel Angel Isla Lucio, Brother Fernando De La Fuente, killed on the same day at the same time at Nyamirangwe in Zaire on October 31st. 1996. The Belgian school principal at Muramba, Griet Bosmans, was killed along with certain students, during the night of April 27-28, 1997. See also where a hundred Rwandan and Burundian, religious men and women and priests were killed as we can find the details on: Http://www.rdrwanda.org./victms/fpr/eglise catholique martyrs. Unfortunately, Death was chained up only for a short time. Death unchained himself and immediately rushed out in the pursuit of, firstly Hutu survivors, then Tutsi survivors.

As a matter of fact, he would gather the spoils in Kigali (capital of Rwanda) especially at Nzove and the surrounding area. The people, fleeing the advancing RPA known as the killing machines, suffered heavy artillery bombardment by troops stationed above them on the hills of Jali, Gisozi, Mount Kigali and Rebero, all the highest points of Kigali. Nzove is a plain, so there the shooters released live shells without meeting any resistance. Death was stationing his soldiers over the entire country, wherever the unlucky Hutu or Tutsi passed. Fierce retribution took place at Goma. Thousands and thousands of Rwandans and Burundians were dying like flies. The reason for the death of an estimated 500,000 victims here is a mystery. Some would say that the cause was a strong poison. Others would say that the culprit was cholera, bloody diarrhea, hunger, fatigue, the oppressive sun, but mostly lack of water for refugees who found themselves on the Kibumba side. They had to travel almost a whole day in search of water. Anyone who was lucky enough to reach the city of Goma would find, not far from the Birere neighborhood, a place nicknamed "The Hutu Place". Here lie the bodies of the Hutu who succumbed to this mysterious sickness. The plight was so traumatic that those who caught this terrible disease would place *themselves* among the bodies in the common graves waiting for the machine that was to bury the bodies. Death still roamed among the Hutu who had remained in the interior of Rwanda, admittedly the true conqueror, always thirsty for more blood and hungry for human flesh. Tens of thousands of Hutu perished in the refugee camp in Kibeho, in southern Rwanda. This camp had harboured a hundred thousand Hutus who had gathered there while fleeing the RPA units who were seeking vengeance on the Hutu population after the Genocide. It was in 1995, just a few months after the attacks and the destruction of the refugee camps, the attacks after which thousands and thousands were massacred in Zaire and Tanzania. Death continued to rage in Zaire.

In the midst of the Tutsi, Death claimed many victims. About a million were killed—I allow my estimation to surpass the official numbers of the ONU who did not take into consideration those who died in circumstances where it was impossible to know where the bodies were hidden or where they died so that they could be counted. This took place over a period of only 100 days. This is what is officially referred to as the Genocide of the Tutsi. As if Death were not yet sated with Tutsi blood, he continued to victimize those in Rwanda's interior, where this time the regulations for order in the interior prevailed. The RPA sought vengeance against the Tutsi who were in Rwanda while they attacked the country from Uganda. Anyone among the Tutsi who had the misfortune of not financially supporting their Army—namely the Tutsi refugees in Uganda for the most part—and who had taken up arms against Rwanda paid for it with blood, his own and that of his loved ones. A similar fate was reserved for anyone who had neglected to send his son or daughter to support the RPA in combat. Today these two categories of Tutsi are still paying the price because it is difficult for them to find suitable employment in current Rwanda. It has become the entitlement of the only Tutsis who returned to Rwanda following their exile in Uganda. This last category got lambasted twice. Their members had been victims of the Hutu extremists who wanted to kill all of them; at the same time, the Tutsi extremists in power today in Rwanda swore to treat them as if they didn't exist. This is why it is not uncommon to hear someone from Uganda ask a refugee—a Tutsi who lived in Rwanda during the attacks and the Genocide—why he hadn't been killed. I find this to be arrogant and doubly cruel.

If we go back to our myth and its application, one could say that, when Sisyphus was captured by Death, Hades had to intervene to have him released. It was only thanks to the intervention of this god that Sisyphus could return to the living. Once he returned to the world of the living, he flatly refused to ever go back to the world of the dead. To Rwandans and Burundians who escaped all the snares of Death personified, I would say that we must all imitate Sisyphus by freeing ourselves of the yoke of Death which has long weighed us down. Similar determination is possible; I firmly believe that. Do you also believe it to be possible? We have repeatedly escaped Death. He stretched out his net to us but we escaped. Bravo! He dug common graves for us, but we refused to go down into them or to make others do so. Bravo! Will this refusal be the fruit of our effort? Not at all! Will it be the fruit of our bravery? Far from it! Were we experts in the art of hiding? A pure lie! Were we able to run faster than those who succumbed? That's a real joke! Let's think of our own people with whom we spent time in the same shelters, in the attics of homes, in the brush, the forest and banana orchards, in the reeds and papyrus grasses, in the rivers and streams, in the plains and swamps, together among the wild beasts, those comrades who are dead while you and I are still alive. We must let ourselves be convinced that staying alive was not the result of happenstance because, as the saying goes *"Akaje gahimwa n'akakazanye"* (what can occur by chance can be destroyed by this same chance).

Based on this principle, I would be already dead. But, if I am still alive, it is because of God's intervention on my behalf. If God allowed the others to leave the face of the earth, it wasn't because

He didn't love them as much, but because He has another plan for you and me: a plan according to the mission that He has designed and assigned to us here on earth. One of the missions is probably to sow peace all over and in so doing be a rock upon which God wants to rebuild unity and fraternity among Burundians, Rwandans, and Congolese. On condition, evidently, of not returning to the world of the dead because there we would be chained up forever.

To give Death yet another opportunity to catch us would make us our own worst enemy. We must deal with what our past has handed down to us as "sub-humans" and fight it relentlessly. To make myself clearly understood, the only and effective truce is the one between humanity and oneself. Do we not say in our own language *"Amahoro y'umutima niwo mutima w'amahoro"* (Peace of the heart is truly the heart of peace)! Thus, if man were to reconcile with himself and throw off the chains of death with which our history has burdened us, he would then be able to sow peace around himself and would cease dealing with all these extremists who sow only terror and death around them. It is through our own peace that others will attain peace, and not the opposite. Mahatma Gandhi liked to say, "Be the peace that you would like to receive from others." If you wait for others to bring you peace, you might die without ever experiencing peace because "even the prettiest girl in the world can only give you what she has," as the French tell us. Who will give you peace when peace is not provided for? Who will give you true peace when it comes at the cost of your own blood? Whoever wants to seek peace at the price of war is a fool.

The period of *"Si vis pacem para bellum"* (If you want peace prepare for war) has devolved because no war occurs without bloodshed, and a bad peace has never existed. If only these bloodthirsty *"hematophiles"* (an expression I have coined to designate "one who can't spend one single night without shedding human blood) and bellicose men of Kigali could understand this and make peace with the Rwandans wherever they might be on our planet—there is no corner of the world where there would not presently be a Rwandan who fled his country because it wanted him dead. It is a pity. One must convince oneself that peace is of the utmost importance. It is the greatest gift that man can give to himself, to his fellow humans, and to all created beings. As far as I know, there has never been a war without bloodshed; peace has never caused anyone any harm. Nothing is better than peace: the inner peace of a person for his own sake and by his own doing, peace for all inhabitants of the whole world, peace for all created beings.

What this describes is a pure Utopia, wouldn't you say? My response is that nothing is impossible for someone who wants to do good. I believe that this is possible, and I am committing myself to it. Let's not forget that a person who doesn't want to make an effort to grow, to become the person he is called to be, becomes instead, more and more etiolated, less of a person. It is solely by entertaining this new way of seeing things, as I am urgently promoting today that Rwandans and Burundians could pass from death to life by sowing life around them, not death and terror. This calls for a change in mentality. We must definitely cut short this "Logic of Death". Why remain prisoners of Death and his acolytes?

A special note: our objective is not to compare the massacre committed by the Hutu against the Tutsi with those of the Tutsi against the Hutu. Far from it! It's all the same to me! We only want to remember that it is in our human nature to protect and to safeguard life. Therefore, considering everything that we have experienced as Rwandans, it is time that we break away from those who continue to offer us death, by pitting us one against the other as a solution to our disputes and a way to manage our differences. It is past time to choose between the two possible paths, life or death. Death has had his turn to reign absolute, so let's allow life to have its turn to act.

Indeed, to live happily and peacefully two things should be avoided: vengeance and violence. There are other misconceptions of which the human mentality should become purified: to believe that we are always right and that others can never be right. To believe that I am worth something and that others are worthless. To believe that I am good and the other person is bad. To lead others to believe that I am the lamb and the other can only always be the wolf. We must absolutely rid ourselves of this exclusivity, a synonym of which seems to be ethnicity, racism, and xenophobia.

Human nature must distance itself from these other concepts which oppose its very essence, namely death and the lie that both of these originate from the "Prince of the World", Death. Each Rwandan, regardless of ethnicity, must break the chain of Death that he or she has carried around the neck for a very long time. Each Rwandan is called to be at the service of truth, the real truth, because lying does not hold true twice as we say in our language, "to the evil-minded one, give a dose and a half of evil." We propose to break the binary logic of Death whose principle is: all or nothing—my ethnicity or none—all power or none at all—everything to be had is mine or no one else's—I am worth everything and you, nothing—I allow myself everything and for you nothing. From this logic, I invite you to move on to the "Logic of the loser is the winner."

This is the art of accepting the other. I accept the other person because he or she has value and is there to complement me, to aid me in my mission on this earth. To live properly is to live for others. To give up something for the good of another is a goal that is difficult to attain. Nevertheless, we must convince ourselves that life consists of losses and gains. We agree to lose or to give up something in order to win something that has a higher value. This logic opposes the desire to dominate, the desire for power that, in this case, consists of wanting to control everything, to suppress everything that you can't control. This new conception of things does not have the docile lamb as a symbol but instead the lion who, assured of his power, agrees not to deploy and unleash his power over the weak ones. The strength of the lion, for we Rwandans, consists in the numerical majority of Hutus at 84% and the minority that we must always protect from power and incessant wars are the Tutsis at 14% and the Batwa at 1%.

If we were to address the two categories of extremists in Rwanda, I would say, "Hématophiles, too much is too much. We have had enough of your blood." Yes, two groups of Rwandan extremists do exist—if we do not count the strangers who claim to be more Hutu or Tutsi than the Hutus or Tutsis themselves. This last group plays the role of catalyst in inter-ethnic violence. The Tutsi extremists flaunt a vengeful hatred of the Hutu, who they say wanted to exterminate all of them. For this group, tolerance and cohabitation are no longer possible. They feel that all the Hutu need to be killed or, at least, as many as possible be eliminated so that the actual number of living Hutu would be less or equal to that of the living Tutsi. This falls in line with the theory of a bloodthirsty high dignitary who said "a barrel full of water, with time, can be drained bone-dry with the help of a little spoon." In other words, everyone who did not ascribe to the ideology of extermination could be eliminated. According to this view, even other Tutsis would be persecuted by this extremist group who thrusts aside others of the same race, denying them the riches of the country because they didn't want to contribute to the diabolic plan to eliminate a large number of the Hutu population. We cannot help but fear the internal conflict between the ruling class in Kigali, nevertheless predominantly Tutsi at this time. Many generals of the regime, at one time well-off, fled the country en masse. Unfortunately, the bloodthirsty regime of Kigali pursues its ex-patriots, even in their country of exile, to kill them. (This is the case in Belgium, South Africa, Norway and lately in Great Britain). We must equally fear what is hiding behind these waves of exiling Tutsi opponents.

As for the Hutu extremists, they have also sworn—and still swear—to the extermination of all Tutsis and any Hutus who get in the way of their extremist ideology. Some dare say that they could never stand alongside a Tutsi. Even if this were to happen by misfortune or necessity they would not speak to each other. Certain occidental countries have offered hospitality to the partisans of this last group. It's unfortunate that they bring their ideology of death into these countries that have a reputation for being peaceful! Some Hutu extremists are still on the lookout in the forests for the least opportunity to plunge the Rwandan people into mourning. I could tell them, "Put down your weapons," we are henceforth thirsty for peace and not for the blood of our compatriots! To all the political parties who are rising up here and there, I would say that all we need is peace and national unity. Rwanda belongs to all of us, Batwa, Hutu, and Tutsi. All ventures that counter this would only lead us to a bloodbath, and we have had enough of that! It is these two types of extremists who bring gloom to Rwanda and who poison the whole Region of the Great Lakes. Such is our history, ancient and recent. Such is our daily life where the drive to dominate is engaged to the fullest. Hundreds of thousands of Tutsi were massacred by Hutu extremists[10] while millions[11] of Hutu were massacred by the Tutsi extremists. Rwanda, because of these extremists, has become the stage for violence and massacres which have plunged the whole Great Lakes Region into mourning. The consequences of these visceral hatreds are multiple: ever-increasing poverty and underdevelopment, incessant deaths and vengeance, the growing number of widows as well as the exorbitant number of orphans and minor-aged children who have become the head of their household, having in their charge other children, minors like themselves. As well, we are experiencing a brain drain; our intellectuals are leaving the country that wants them dead to go to foreign countries. Think about this if you still love your country!

To restore peace in the country—and in the Great Lakes Region—is only a possibility if we master our prejudices and embark on a path of honest dialogue with each other, a dialogue blind to numerical superiority and one which concerns itself with the future rather than the past, a dialogue wherein all parties have a voice.

There must be an intermediary group, one who allows others to speak and to express themselves. In doing so, they could exchange among themselves the best of what they have to offer. I believe that is true "democracy" as the Greeks first conceived it. The "Logic of the loser is the winner" proposes this last plan as the only way out. To you who insist on clinging to your extremism, you will reap only misery and death. As for myself, strong in my convictions that I am

10   Numbers range from 500,000 to 1.5 million victims in 1994. (cf. Filip Reyntjens, "Estimation of the number of people killed in Rwanda in 1994" in the Annuaires des Grands Lacs (Great Lakes Yearbook) 1996-1997, Harmattan, Paris, 1997 p. 179-186).

11   The true number of Hutus killed by the RPF in the interior of Rwanda in 1994 is far from known. Read the Gersony Report, Op. cit. See also Abdul Joshua Ruzibiza, Op. cit. According to him, the number of civilian Hutus killed by the RPF in the same period of 1994 rises to 450,000. See also, HRW/FIDH, No witness can survive, LE GENOCIDE AU RWANDA (The Rwandan Genocide) Karthala, 1999, p. 842-852.

sharing with you today, I know that I may be counted among your future victims because of what I have just proposed. But know that, at least, I will have shown you a path to life, a path allowing you to escape the mesh of death and the cycle of violence that chains you to that state of existence. Dead or alive, I will have introduced you to a civilized lifestyle. In our father's language, I say to you *"Va i buzimu, dore i buntu. Gira impagarike y'ubugingo"* (Leave behind your world of Death and come back to life. Live life, an authentic life, to the fullest!)

ACRONYMS

AFLD – Alliance of Democratic Forces for the Liberation of the Congo

FARG – Funds for Genocide Survivors

HCR – High Commission for Refugees

RAF – Rwandan Armed Forces

RPA – Rwandan Patriotic Army

RPF – Rwandan Patriotic Front

UNAMIR –United Nations Assistance Mission for Rwanda

UNHCR – United Nations High Commission For Refugees

UNZCCS – United Nations Zairian Contingent for Camp Security

ZAF – Zairian Armed Forces

CPSIA information can be obtained at www.ICGtesting.com
Printed in the USA
LVOW091458010412

275518LV00001B/4/P